DON'T INVITE THEM TO CHURCH

Moving From a Come and See
to a GO AND BE CHURCH

KAREN WILK

Printed in the United States of America.

Library of Congress Cataloging-in-Publication Data
Wilk, Karen.
    Don't invite them to church : moving from a come and see to a go and be church / by Karen Wilk.
      p. cm.
    ISBN 978-1-59255-531-4
    1. Evangelistic work—Textbooks. 2. Communities—Religious aspects—Christianity—Textbooks
    3. Neighborliness—Religious aspects—Christianity—Textbooks.teaching. I. Title.
    BV3793.W475 2010
    248'.5—dc22

2010023661

Mixed Sources
Product group from well-managed forests and other controlled sources
www.fsc.org Cert no. SW-COC-002283
© 1996 Forest Stewardship Council
FSC

10 9 8 7 6 5 4 3 2 1

Contents

Dedication

This guidebook is dedicated to all those who long for something more:

- to see God's kingdom come
- to live out the "sentness" of God's calling
- to experience true community in keeping the Great Commission and the two greatest commandments

It's for those who long for the courage and conviction to become who God made them to be, to be the presence of Jesus where they are, and to join the myriad people throughout the centuries who counted the cost and sold everything.

—KW

Acknowledgments

This book grew out of *Living Dangerously,* an eight-week guide designed and written for The River Community Church in Edmonton, Alberta. I am grateful to those who engaged in that journey in the fall of 2009. Their input and participation helped reshape the material into its current form. Their stories also enrich and concretize the principles and pursuits described here. Particular thanks go to people who stepped up and stepped out and are now on the journey in their neighborhoods, where every day affords a new adventure as they partner with God in bringing his kingdom near!

Special thanks also to the staff and leadership of The River Community Church who dedicated several months of the church year to this endeavor, preached a number of messages in connection with it, and allowed their hearts and lives to be shaped by it. Podcasts of those Sunday morning messages can be found on the church's website at www.rivercommunity.ca.

Howard Lawrence, director of Neighborhood Life for Forge Canada and a "lifer" in neighborhood groups, also contributed to this book through his passion, wisdom, commitment, and experience. Without him going before us and encouraging us, this project would hardly have been possible. In the same way, I want to thank Forge Canada and in particular its national director, Cam Roxburgh, who got many of us committed to the missional church conversation and practice.

Finally, I'd like to thank my courageous and committed husband, Steve, who has been an amazingly willing participant and partner as we have sought to live out this journey, and who gave up lots of "personal vegging out" time for the sake of the kingdom and for love of neighbor.

—Karen Wilk

Introduction

As I was typing away the other day, my daughter asked me what the name of this book was. I told her, and she replied, "What does that mean?" I asked, "What do you think it means?" She said, "I know what it means, Mom: you don't want Christians to invite people to church, you want them to love their neighbors and *be* the church."

Wow. At age thirteen, she gets it. In three words, that is what this book is about: loving our neighbors.

So if a thirteen-year-old gets it, why do we need a whole guidebook devoted to loving our neighbors? Because, truthfully, most of us aren't doing it very well. Knowing those three words as the second greatest commandment doesn't mean we know how to live them actively, faithfully, and intentionally.

In this book we'll wrestle with the practical meaning of loving our neighbors. We'll ask questions like these:

- What if there is something more to the Second Commandment than just trying to be "nice" to everyone?
- What if you actually loved your neighbor and were the presence of Jesus where you live, where God has placed you right now?
- What if believers who lived in the same neighborhood formed a *communitas* (a community with a mission) right where they lived, whose purpose was to make their neighborhood a place where the values of God's kingdom become more visible and real . . . and others noticed and wanted to be part of it?

This book raises questions, makes confessions, and seeks answers. But mostly it invites you to pursue the calling and challenge of loving your neighbor, not just with words but in postures and practices.

Jesus used this illustration: "The kingdom of heaven is like yeast that a woman took and mixed into about sixty pounds of flour until it worked all through the dough" (Matt. 13:33). As we seek to live out our love for our neighbors, perhaps, like yeast in dough, we will have more impact than we might ever imagine. Perhaps we will experience God's kingdom come in new and astonishing ways. Perhaps some dough will rise.

How to Use This Guidebook

Don't Invite Them to Church is designed to help you, your small group, or your whole church learn what it truly means to love your neighbors. It's designed, as the subtitle says, to help you move from being a "come and see" church to a "go and be" church. It's about becoming missional people whose daily walk matches our talk.

If you work through this guidebook as a congregation or a small group, the intent is that you meet together as a group once a week for eight weeks. In these group sessions you'll encourage each other, tell your stories, and learn how to better love your neighbor.

Here's how this guidebook is organized:

Stories from the Journey
God is taking my family and me on a journey into neighborhood living. Each week begins with a story from that journey. While my story is different from your story, my hope is that our adventures will help you begin to imagine and grapple with your own expedition into neighborhood life as you pursue the journey yourself and with your group.

Pursuits of the Week
Each week you'll practice four "pursuits" (see p. 10 for in-depth information about each of these):

- ▣ Sideward (group meeting)—grow with the members of your group and reflect together on missional living
- ⌃ Upward—grow in your personal relationship with God
- ◂ Inward—grow in your own spiritual life
- ▶ Outward—grow in your love for neighbor

Time with God's Word: Day 1 of each week will be your group meeting. For Days 2-7, we provide devotional readings, experiences in spiritual disciplines, and thought questions to help you on your journey.

Life Stories and Quotables

In this guidebook you will also find true-life stories from your sisters and brothers who have begun to step out into neighborhood life. We hope these stories will inspire, motivate, and empower you to do the same.

Throughout, you will also find Quotables, which are tidbits of wisdom and experience from the "experts" who have been pursuing missional church for a long time. They are there for you to ponder on your own and with your group.

Each of the components described above has the same goal: equipping, empowering, and encouraging you to love your neighbor and be the presence of Jesus—his kingdom come—in your neighborhood. Like any important practice, they will require some time, effort, and attention.

As you come to the end of this guidebook, your group can continue to shape its life together around the four pursuits (see Next Steps), supporting, encouraging, and loving one another "that others might know."

I am so thankful and excited that you are joining this journey of rediscovering the art and the power of good neighboring. As Paul said to the Thessalonians, "May the Lord make your love increase and overflow for each other and for everyone else, just as ours does for you" (1 Thess. 3:12).

If you have comments, questions, stories to share, or would like me to come alongside you or your group or congregation in other ways, please feel free to contact me at karen.wilk@forge canada.ca.

The Pursuits: Practices and Postures

As mentioned previously, each week you'll practice four "pursuits"—practices to shape your living as you grow in love for your small group, your God, yourself, and your neighbor.

⬎ Sideward Pursuits

"Be devoted to one another in love" (Rom. 12:10).

The first pursuit each week is the side-by-side (or "sideward") pursuit, otherwise known as your group meeting time. This is your opportunity to get to know each other better, discuss, share, and pray about what you've learned the week before. During the group meeting you'll also look ahead to the pursuits you'll practice on your own during the coming week.

The material for these gatherings is designed to help you grow together as a group. It includes community-building suggestions and discussion questions. The goal of your weekly gathering, however, is not to "get through the questions." The goal is personal and communal nurture and engagement. Make the most of this opportunity to connect, support each other, bless and be blessed, and pray with and for one another and your neighbors.

As you begin this journey, commit to participating every week, to sharing honestly, and to pushing each other to fuller life in community.

⬆ Upward Pursuits

"Jesus replied, 'Love the Lord your God with all your heart and with all your soul and with all your mind. This is the first and greatest commandment'" (Matt. 22:37-38).

In keeping with the first and greatest commandment, we need to engage in upward pursuits that draw us into a closer relationship with God. There are many such practices: prayer, meditating on Scripture, and silence, to a name a few. We'll progress through eight such postures and practices to help us walk with Jesus as his sent people.

◀ Inward Pursuits

"And we all, who with unveiled faces contemplate the Lord's glory, are being transformed into his image with ever-increasing glory, which comes from the Lord, who is the Spirit" (2 Cor. 3:18).

As we move upward and sideward, God reshapes us and helps us conform more and more to the image of Christ. The inward pursuits in this guidebook focus on the character traits of mature believers as recorded in 2 Peter 1:3-8. God longs for us to be holy as he is holy. Christ calls us to be imitators of him. Our character, integrity, and authenticity are critical to our witness, because we are the light of the world (Matt. 5:14).

▶ Outward Pursuits

"And the second is like it: 'Love your neighbor as yourself'" (Matt. 22:37).

The fourth pursuit is the outward one. This pursuit gives us tangible ways to keep the second great commandment. One of the amazing realities of this posture and practice is that it's actually great fun and very rewarding. Neighbors *like* connecting and getting to know each other. They also like serving and sharing and feeling that they belong and matter.

As we engage in outward pursuits, we also find ourselves engaging in the Great Commission without turning people into projects and making them and ourselves uncomfortable. That is one of the most exciting and enjoyable parts of starting this journey. The pressure's off! Your mission, your calling, is simply to love your neighbors—not to get them to attend church, say a certain prayer, confess, profess, renounce, or repent. That's God's work. Your work is to testify in word and deed to God's love. As you do that, you'll find that the Spirit does marvelous things.

Time with God's Word

"... My word that goes out from my mouth ... will not return to me empty, but will accomplish what I desire and achieve the purpose for which I sent it" (Isa. 55:11).

Willow Creek's recent study of 80,000 people in 200 congregations found that the best catalyst for spiritual growth, whether for explorers or for committed Christ-centered people, is reflection on God's Word. So this guidebook includes "Time with God's Word": passages from the Bible related to the weekly theme, along with reflection questions.

Since Day 1 of the week is reserved for your group meeting, the Time with God's Word section begins on Day 2 of each week. Day 2 always includes a brief reflection to take you deeper into the theme of the week. You may choose to read and think about it on it on Day 2, or whenever you have a little more time to reflect on the text.

In any case, take your time in God's Word. Try to set aside at least fifteen minutes each day to pray, meditate, and reflect. Many Christians find that their reflection on the Word is enhanced when they journal—an ancient practice of writing down responses, prayers, thoughts, and feelings. Something seems to happen (the Spirit moves/speaks?) when we actually record what's happening inside, and it's always enlightening to look back and see how God has been at work.

If you wish, you can reflect on Time with God's Word with a friend, a spouse, or your family. If you do this, be sure everyone has a chance to process and respond.

GO BACK—I AM SENDING YOU!

Stories from the Journey

My family's journey started when my husband, Steve, and I decided to truly connect with our neighbors. We were acquainted with a few of them primarily through our kids' activities, but there was little more to our relationships. Our children went to a Christian school and we were very involved in our church (after all, I am a pastor). Who had the time or energy for neighbors? Truth be told, we were more likely to avoid talking to our neighbors (we had things to do, places to go, people to see) than we were to stop and visit with them.

But after a while you have to pay attention to the angst in your soul. Something was missing. Even though we were part of what most would call a "successful church plant" shaped on the missional model, I wasn't sure we were really connecting with the people we lived near who needed to know how much God loved them and how good his kingdom is.

If God is a sending God and we are his sent ones, surely that must mean more than inviting people to church or to "our" events, programs, and services—no matter how great they are. Can the light, the salt, the sweet aroma of Christ really expect the darkness, the unpreserved, and those who long for a better smell, *to come to them*?

Of course, I wasn't thinking about any of this on the December evening when I was designing and printing invitations to our family's first Christmas Open House. I was thinking about whether anyone in our neighborhood would come and what I should serve and how awkward the silences might be. Still, we folded the colorful invitations and put them in the mailboxes of everyone on our street (because we were too chicken to knock on their doors).

The day arrived, the house was decorated, and the table was spread with sweet treats, appetizers, Christmas punch, hot apple cider, and more. The first couple rang the doorbell and before the woman had her coat off and we had introduced ourselves she blurted out, "We just had to come to see who would do such a thing—inviting strangers into their home!"

And so began our journey into the joy and richness of neighborhood life.

◩ Sideward Pursuit (Group Meeting): Welcome One Another

BEING COMMUNITY

"So reach out and welcome one another to God's glory. Jesus did it; now *you* do it!" (Rom. 15:7, *The Message*).

When a group like yours starts out on a new adventure with a new commitment, there is usually both anticipation and some fear or anxiety. So have a welcome celebration! This week's gathering is meant to build a sense of community by the power of a warm welcome. It's a theme that resonates throughout Scripture as we hear the call to extend hospitality and to celebrate together the goodness of God and the life he gives us.

Make your first get-together one of food and fun. Try a potluck, an international dinner, a progressive dinner, or a "make your own sundae" (everyone brings a topping). Have a campfire. Play some icebreaker games. Do whatever you think will make people feel welcome and comfortable.

Christians should never underestimate the value of a good party, by the way. Jesus did his first miracle at a wedding party (John 2:1-10). He was anointed for his burial at a dinner party (Luke 7:36-50). The Pharisees criticized Jesus because they thought he was too much of a "partier" (Luke 7:34). When Jesus spoke of the kingdom of heaven, he called it a banquet (Luke 14:15-24). When a sinner repents, heaven throws a party (Luke 15:5-7, 9-10, 22-24).

INTRODUCE THE JOURNEY

- Before your first gathering, invite participants to read through the introductory pages of this guidebook.
- After your welcome celebration, give everyone an opportunity to share why they joined this group and what they hope to get out of this journey together.
- Take some time to review the format of this guidebook and its relationship to the group meeting. If participants did not receive their guidebooks prior to this gathering, read through the opening pages together.

PREPARE FOR THE PURSUITS OF THE WEEK

- Introduce and discuss each of the other postures and practices for this week:

    ⬆ **Upward:** Breath Prayer

    ⬅ **Inward:** Faith

    ➡ **Outward:** Identifying your Neighborhood/Missional Context
- Pose these questions: Which of these pursuits will be most challenging for you? What are you looking forward to? How can your group support/pray for you as you begin the adventure of learning to love your neighbors?
- Pray for one another and your neighborhoods.

───────────────────

Practice the following upward, inward, and outward pursuits on your own this week. Plan to complete them before your next group meeting.

⬆ Upward Pursuit: **Breath Prayer**

"Jesus replied, 'Love the Lord your God with all your heart and with all your soul and with all your mind. This is the first and greatest commandment'" (Matt. 22:37-38).

We begin our upward pursuit by learning to pause and become more aware of God's constant presence with us. "I am with you" was the promise and assurance of God's presence made not only to Moses, but to saints throughout the ages. It was affirmed again in Jesus' parting words, "I am with you always" (Matt. 28:20).

Set aside some time each day to open your heart to God by praying a "Breath Prayer." A good time to take this posture is right before you do the "Time with God's Word" exercises (see pp. 21-26). Here's how to practice this type of prayer:

- Get into a comfortable but alert position, sitting with your hands in your lap, palms upward (an open, receptive posture).
- Close your eyes and relax your whole body, starting with your feet and moving up to your head. Be still.
- Focus on your breathing. Don't *change* your breathing, just be aware of it. If (or when) your mind wanders, gently bring it back to your breathing. Clear everything else from your mind for now.
- Repeat this line over and over again as you breathe in and out: *Breathe on me, breath of God, breathe on me.*
- While you are breathing in, imagine God's breath—his Spirit, his love, his power, his presence—filling you. Inhale God's grace and peace. Exhale your sins, pain, fear, and doubt. Visualize them being carried away on the breath of God. Stay in this awareness with every breath. Try this for about two minutes.

As the practice of Breath Prayer becomes more familiar to you, you can use it anytime and anywhere. For more on the breath of God, check out Genesis 2:7; Job 32:8; 33:4; Acts 17:28; John 15:4, 7, 9.

Inward Pursuit: Faith

"His divine power has given us everything we need for a godly life through our knowledge of him who called us by his own glory and goodness. Through these he has given us his very great and precious promises, so that through them you may participate in the divine nature, having escaped the corruption in the world caused by evil desires. For this very reason, make every effort to add to your faith goodness; and to goodness, knowledge; and to knowledge, self-control; and to self-control, perseverance; and to perseverance, godliness; and to godliness, mutual affection; and to mutual affection, love. For if you possess these qualities in increasing measure, they will keep you from being ineffective and unproductive in your knowledge of our Lord Jesus Christ" (2 Pet. 1:3-8).

Read the above passage several times. Each week we will strive to understand and live out one of the characteristics listed in it. The starting place for "participants in the divine nature" is our faith. So focus on your faith this week.

Faith has been described as BELIEF + TRUST + ACTION. Think and/or journal about the following questions:

- How's your believing?
- Do you really trust God? Recall (and journal about) some examples.
- Are you acting on what you know, living every day as a "sent one" because you're confident in God?
- Are you faith-*full*?
- What would have to happen for you to grow in faith?
- What might the Lord be asking you to commit to or receive now, so that your faith might be the grounding for a character molded in Christ's character?

As you evaluate your faith, be assured that your relationship with God is not dependent on *your* faith. Jesus declares that if we have faith as small as a mustard seed, we will be able to move mountains, and nothing(!) will be impossible for us (Matt. 17:20). In other words, the size of our faith does not determine the outcomes—God does. By his grace and mighty power, mountains are moved and hearts are changed, even ours. Praise God!

▶ Outward Pursuit: Identifying Your Neighborhood

"Forced to leave home base, the followers of Jesus all became missionaries. Wherever they were scattered, they preached the Message about Jesus" (Acts 8:4, *The Message*).

As explained in the introduction, this guidebook isn't just for *learning about* "missional incarnational living" and loving our neighbors, it's about *doing* it!

Here is your first challenge: acknowledging where God has placed you. Where we dwell is our primary missional context, as it was for Jesus and his first followers in the young church. We are the presence of Jesus where we live.

Your missional context—your neighborhood—is where your interactions are "S-A-F-E":

S: Spontaneous—A missional context is a place where we have spontaneous connections with others, such as over the fence, while walking the dog, at the grocery store or gym, wherever we "bump into" each other.

A: Accessible—A neighborhood is a place where we are easily accessible to one another. For example, we can walk across the street or across the hall to borrow a cup of sugar, or call to let each other know when the garage door has been left open.

F: Frequent—In order to nurture relationships, your neighborhood boundaries will identify people whom you encounter (or could encounter) regularly.

E: at Ease—There is something unique about a neighborhood. We live there! And so does God. We are called to be salt and light on our street, where we live among our neighbors. People need to see and know real-life Christ-followers living authentically and genuinely right next door. They see us "with our hair down"—interacting with our kids, taking out the garbage in our bathrobe, and so on. Your neighborhood is the community in which you are present "as you are."

Based on these parameters, jot down the "boundaries" of your neighborhood. As you go and grow, you may find that God will enlarge your neighborhood, but for now start with those immediately around you.

> **"We cannot minimize [missional living] as something that is simply part of the church's task. It *is* the church's task."**
>
> (from "The Missional Church in Suburbia," a paper by Todd Hiestand, posted on www.toddhiestand.com)

"The Word became flesh and blood, and moved into the neighborhood. We saw the glory with our own eyes, the one-of-a-kind glory, like Father, like Son, generous inside and out, true from start to finish" (John 1:14, *The Message*).

Describe and map your neighborhood—the place where you can develop **S**pontaneous, **A**ccessible, **F**requent, and at **E**ase relationships. Diagram it with little houses, and on each house write the names of the people (and pets) who live there and anything else that you know about those neighbors (work, hobbies, needs). Talk with God, your spouse, and/or other believers in your neighborhood, and be prepared to share what you learned at your next group gathering.

LIFE STORY

I committed to working through the booklet *Praying the Lord's Prayer for Neighbors* for my daily devotions. It suggests that you pick five neighbors on your street and pray for them. I did this. I was amazed when the people across the street (one of my five) then showed up at one of our Sunday morning services. When I talked to them, they told me that they were looking for a church home and were checking us out! —KG

TIME WITH GOD'S WORD

Theme for the Week: Sending

"[God said] 'It's time for you to go back: I'm sending you to Pharaoh to bring my people, the People of Israel, out of Egypt.' Moses answered God, 'But why me? What makes you think that I could ever go to Pharaoh and lead the children of Israel out of Egypt?' 'I'll be with you,' God said. 'And this will be the proof that I am the one who sent you: When you have brought my people out of Egypt, you will worship God right here at this very mountain'" (Ex. 3:10-12, *The Message*).

Do words on the pages of Scripture ever suddenly leap out at you, even in a passage that you have read a hundred times before? That happened to me when I read this passage.

God interrupted Moses' daily routines, his retirement plans, his timelines, with a directive: "Go back. I am sending you."

Moses wasn't so sure about God's suggested course of action—why would he want to "go back"? Moses was in a place that for forty years had provided him with a safe, secure, predictable environment in the sheltered community of his father-in-law, Jethro. Why would he want to go back to Egypt, where he would be uncomfortable, at risk, and confronted with change? For Moses, it was a moment that would alter the trajectory of his life.

So Moses hesitated. He told God, "I can't do something like that! Really, I just can't. Are you sure you want me?"

"Yes," God said, "I am sending you."

This sending is a word for us too. But why would the church want to go back? Why would we want to give up comfort, security, stability, familiarity, control, predictability, and routine for the uncomfortable, risky, unconventional, dangerous, challenging, unpredictable adventure of being sent to be a blessing?

That's why those words jumped out at me. They fit with what God has been stirring up in my heart and mind—unsettling me and my understanding of what it means to be church.

Traditional churches are declining, denominations are losing their voice in society, cathedrals are closing, more and more people seem to be turned off by the institutional church, which once held prominence and loyalty. What is God up to? Can the message really be "Go back"?

Even seeker-sensitive, outreach-focused churches like the one I am a part of, which do everything possible to attract newcomers and make seekers feel welcome and embraced, are beginning to wonder.

Why? Because no matter how attractive we are and how many times we invite them, the people across the street who don't know Jesus and his love aren't coming. Maybe we've made it all too complicated: trying to design the perfect programs, the best worship services, the biggest youth events, the most fun children's activities.

"Go back, I am sending you . . . ." That's what the blazing bush in my corner of the world seems to be saying, and those words stop me in my tracks. The God who speaks from burning bushes and through still small voices and mighty winds and angels is the sending God.

God sent Abraham and Esther and Ruth and Deborah and Joshua and Jonah and all the prophets—and then God the Father sent the Son. After the Son died and rose again, he and the Father sent the Spirit. And now the Spirit sends us.

We're sent to go and make disciples—not just to reach out but to *go out*. The sending God is the one who seeks and saves the lost. He doesn't wait for them or seek to attract them to his program. He goes out after them.

Day 2

"I delight in your decrees; I will not neglect your word" (Ps. 119:16).

Practice the Breath Prayer (p. 16).

If you haven't already, read the theme reflection (p. 21). Then explore these questions:

- What parts of this reflection spoke to you? Why?
- What might God be saying to you, your group, or your church through the reflection?
- What does it mean to you that we are a "sent people"?
- What might be a first step for you in rethinking your identity and calling as "a sent one"? When will you take it?

Talk with God about what you're hearing, thinking, wrestling with, and enjoying so far in this study.

Day 3

"I delight in your decrees; I will not neglect your word" (Ps. 119:16).

Practice the Breath Prayer.

Then read Matthew 10:1-7 and explore these questions:

- What did Jesus do for/with his disciples?
- As you review the names of the disciples, what strikes you about Jesus' followers?
- What does it mean for you to be called, given authority, and sent this week?
- How might God want you to "go and announce" that "the kingdom of God is near" in your neighborhood? What will you do to respond?

Pray for a greater understanding of who you are, as well as who you are called, equipped, and sent to be as a follower of Jesus.

Day 4

"I delight in your decrees; I will not neglect your word" (Ps. 119:16).

Practice the Breath Prayer.

Then read Matthew 10:8-15 and explore these questions:
- List the do's and don'ts of Jesus' instructions. How might they apply to his followers today?
- From whom might God want you to accept hospitality? How?
- To whom might God want you to give your blessing?
- What will you "give as freely as you have received" today?

Sing or say as a prayer the old song "Freely, Freely (God Forgave My Sin)," which is based on this passage (lyrics available at www.audiblefaith.com). Then turn it into your prayer for the day.

Day 5

"I delight in your decrees; I will not neglect your word" (Ps. 119:16).

Practice the Breath Prayer.

Then read Matthew 10:16-23 and explore these questions:
- When have you felt like a sheep among wolves? How was that feeling related to (or not related to) your faith?
- How might being a Jesus-follower require being like a snake? Like a dove?
- How do you feel about the opportunities God might give you to act like a sheep, snake, or dove?
- What encourages you in this passage?

Pray about your witness and testimony as you go about your daily life this week and as you identify the boundaries of your neighborhood.

Day 6

"I delight in your decrees; I will not neglect your word" (Ps. 119:16).

Practice the Breath Prayer.

Then read Matthew 10:24-42 and explore these questions:
- How are you like your Teacher and Master? How not?
- What are you most afraid of when it comes to "declaring"?
- How does Jesus address this fear (and others)?
- How do you interpret Jesus' words in verses 34-39? How do you apply them?
- How do you interpret Jesus' words in verses 40-42? How do you apply them?
- Imagine that you are one of the first disciples receiving these instructions from Jesus. How do you respond?

Talk to the Lord about what you've been hearing.

Pray for one specific way to "acknowledge" Jesus (v. 32) before others today and ask God to give you the courage and the opportunity to do it.

Share your experiences with your group.

Day 7

"I delight in your decrees; I will not neglect your word" (Ps. 119:16).

Practice the Breath Prayer.

Then read Matthew 28:1-10 and explore these questions:
- What three things are the women told to do?
- Reflect on your own experiences of "coming and seeing" the risen Lord.
- How might we "come and see" the risen Lord today?
- How have you or do you "go quickly and tell"?

- How can you as a group "come and see" and "go and tell" *together* and help others to do the same? Try to think of some specific suggestions. As the angel said, "Do not be afraid." In other words, *go for it, and quickly!*

At your next group meeting, be prepared to share your "outward' pursuit"—your S-A-F-E context (see p. 19)—and what you have been learning and experiencing about your neighborhood throughout the week.

LIFE STORY

As I began to think of myself as a sent one, I began asking myself, "What's God's dream for our neighborhood?" This changed everything for me. It set me free and filled me with wonder so that as I walked to the grocery store (which I am doing more often now for this very reason), as I worked in the garden, and as I went in and out in my ordinary way, I was constantly in conversation with God about what he desires for my neighborhood. I imagined all the things that could happen to make us a community . . . street parties, outdoor movie nights (our garage door makes a great screen), gatherings in our family room, games, tea time. It's wonderful! —LF

STEP INTO NEIGHBORHOOD LIFE

Stories from the Journey

We had a wonderful time at our Christmas Open House and have had many neighborhood gatherings since then. We have hosted monthly bridge parties; wine, cheese, and art nights; backyard barbeques and campfires; and international dinners. Our neighbors have hosted various gatherings too. It's been great fun to get to know them and begin to trust, care for, and depend on each other as neighbors.

We do all these things without another agenda, which is why we can relax and develop relationships. We don't love our neighbors so that we can invite them to church. In fact, we have discovered great freedom and joy in loving our neighbors because God is already there among them.

When we began to pray for our neighbors regularly, the evidence that God was going ahead of us just kept coming and coming. We had had several women's gatherings—a get-together to celebrate a retirement, a tea, a girls' night to trade clothes and jewelry, and so on. I felt the Spirit's nudging to follow that up; what if we had these "teas" on a regular basis? So I made a deal with God—I needed assurance for taking this step of faith, and God humored me. I prayed that if God really wanted me to gather the women in our neighborhood regularly, then when I suggested the idea to my neighbors, God would "prove it" with at least three "yes" responses from them.

I bumped into one neighbor when we were both walking our respective dogs, and we started chatting. I said something like, "You know, I have really enjoyed our neighborhood teas." "Me too," she said. I said, "I've been wondering if anyone might be interested in having them more regularly, like maybe every other Friday morning." She said, "That would be really good. I would definitely come." A few days later I was chatting with another neighbor and the conversation went a similar way. And, you guessed it, the third woman I talked with was also very positive about the idea.

So now we've been having "Tea at Ten" about every other week. God is taking the conversations deeper and we are getting to know each other better. We've talked about the hurt that some of us have experienced in our family of origin. We've talked about reincarnation and contemplative dialogue. We had three new people last time, and God is in our midst *every time*.

WEEK 2 PURSUITS ⬗ ⌃ ⟨ ⟩

⬗ Sideward Pursuit (Group Meeting): Live in Harmony with One Another

BEING COMMUNITY

- Enjoy refreshments together.
- Build community by talking about the subject of harmony. Invite everyone to tell a story about a bad date (or another get-together) where there was little or no harmony.
- Alternatively, invite everyone to describe how harmony is evident or not in their family of origin.

REVIEW WEEK 1

Reflect on the postures and practices from Week 1 with the following questions. Make sure everyone has a chance to share. If your group is large (more than eight) divide into smaller units of two to four each (especially if you are likely to run out of meeting time).

- ⬗ **Sideward:** After meeting people during last week's group meeting, how are you feeling about participating in this group?
- ⌃ **Upward:** What was practicing the Breath Prayer like for you?
- ⟨ **Inward:** How did you describe your faith?
- ⟩ **Outward:** After you identified the boundaries of your neighborhood, your missional context, what have you noticed God doing in response to that identification, either in you or in your neighborhood?

DISCUSS THIS WEEK'S THEME

One of the passages in this week's Time with God's Word is Philippians 2, where Paul highlights Jesus' humility and calls us to imitate him. It takes humility to get along and to live in harmony with others. Being together requires give and take, good communication, humbling ourselves so that we are quick to listen. Being community also calls for intentionality. So be intentional as a group by discussing how you will "live in harmony" with one another. Consider each other's expectations and needs in terms of

- meeting times and locations.
- attendance and participation.
- refreshments.
- leadership (one appointed leader, or shared responsibility).
- sharing, praying, and confidentiality.

You may want to write down what you decide so that anyone can refer back to what you agreed, if necessary.

PREPARE FOR THE PURSUITS OF THE WEEK

Introduce and discuss the other postures and practices for Week 2.

⬆ **Upward:** Open Hands

◀ **Inward:** Goodness

▶ **Outward:** Praying that God will "B-L-E-S-S" our neighbors

- What will be most challenging for you?
- What are you looking forward to?
- How can your group support and pray for you as you engage in these postures and practices this week?

Pray for one another and your neighborhoods.

Practice the following upward, inward, and outward pursuits on your own this week. Plan to complete them before your next group meeting.

⬆ Upward Pursuit: **Open Hands**

You may want to continue to practice the Breath Prayer as you did last week.

This week as you pause and acknowledge God's presence, also indicate your desire and openness to hearing and receiving from God what he has for you. Remember that God loves you, knows you by name, and wants to be in relationship with you.

One posture from the Bible (see 2 Chron. 6:12; Lam. 3:41) that represents our willingness to be open to God is opening our hands.

In a comfortable sitting position, open your hands as if someone were about to place something in them or raise your hands toward God and concentrate on your open palms. Imagine that your hands represent your prayer (your conversation with God) right now.

- What are you giving to God? What are you inviting God to take away?
- What is God placing in your hands? Why? What does God want you to receive from him or hear from him?

Try not to talk or think too much; simply wait for God to speak to you. Try this several times throughout the week and journal about it here.

"The whole point of what we're urging is simply *love*—love uncontaminated by self-interest and counterfeit faith, a life open to God" (1 Tim. 1:5, *The Message*).

Inward Pursuit: Goodness

"For this very reason, make every effort to add to your faith goodness" (2 Pet. 1:5).

What does it mean to be good, or to add goodness to your faith?

Most of the time when we find the word "good" or "goodness" used in the Bible, it's in reference to God's goodness, which blesses and frees us. (Check out 2 Chron. 6:41; Neh. 9:35; Ps. 23:6; 27:13; 119:40; 145:7; Isa. 63:7; Hosea 3:5; Acts 14:17; 1 Pet. 2:9.) How have you experienced God's goodness?

After Pentecost, the Bible begins to assign this attribute to people, because people filled with the Holy Spirit bear the fruit of the Spirit, including goodness (Gal. 5:22).

What might goodness have to do with your missional calling, incarnational living, and neighborhood context? This week be good to someone
- in your workplace or school,
- in your family,
- in your group or the bigger church community, and
- in your neighborhood context.

Share your experiences at your next group meeting so you can build each other up!

Outward Pursuit: Pray for Your Neighbors

You might not think of prayer as an outward pursuit, but when we pray for those among whom God has placed us, there is outward movement. Prayer moves the hands of God.

While on vacation, we prayed for opportunities to make personal connections with some of our neighbors. The first evening we were home, I was talking over the fence to my single neighbor and invited her to join us for a burger . . . and she did!

The next day another neighbor arrived at our door, asking if she could use our phone, as hers was not working. We had tea for an hour and a half. That same evening, we were invited for pizza at a neighbor's home! God loves to respond to these prayers, so be prepared! His answers may come sooner than you think.

This week, identify and pray for at least five households in your neighborhood every day. Try using the acronym B-L-E-S-S. This of course, may require you to connect in some "S-A-F-E" ways with your neighbors (see Week 1's outward pursuit on p. 19) so that you can learn more about who they are, what they do, their family, and so on, in order to pray for them meaningfully.

Pray that God would B-L-E-S-S your neighbors. Pray for their
Body (health, strength, protection)
Labor (work, income, security, school)
Emotional state (joy, peace, hope, contentment, fulfillment, self-esteem)
Social life (relationships, love, marriage, family, friends)
Spiritual needs (grace, openness, hunger for God, faith)

Pray this prayer aloud:
> Lord, be Lord of this neighborhood. Show yourself in ways that are far greater then we could ever ask or imagine. Help us to see you in everyone we meet and experience you in our midst, so that at the name of Jesus every knee should bow, and every tongue confess in our neighborhood, that you, Jesus, are Lord—to the glory of God the Father. Amen.

TIME WITH GOD'S WORD

Theme for the Week: Jesus, the Lord, Walks with Us

"As they talked and discussed these things with each other, Jesus himself came up and walked along with them . . ." (Luke 24:15).

The story of the disciples walking to Emmaus after Jesus' resurrection (Luke 24:13-35) stands out as an example of what it means to be missional and incarnational. We usually hear this story at Easter and then dive right into the ham and chocolate! But if we pause and imagine the scene, if we "live into" it, it provides a word for us as we seek to be good friends and neighbors.

Two disciples walk along the dusty road to the village of Emmaus, heads down, shoulders slumped, feet dragging— even though they're talking about Jesus. Of course, that's because they are talking about a *dead* Jesus. I imagine it all happening in slow motion. If you have lost a loved one, you know what it's like. For a time, the whole world is a blur and you just go through the motions.

Suddenly Jesus comes up and starts walking with them, listening to their story, feeling their pain and confusion. He responds to their need to understand the events that so bewilder them. So Jesus patiently explains the Scriptures to them from the beginning. He assures them that what has happened was God's plan from the beginning—that even when everything around them seems totally lost, God is still in control.

The disciples need to get their heads out of the dust and their eyes off their feet. They need to discover that Jesus is walking beside them.

The longer they are with him, the more their hearts thaw until, when they receive the bread from Jesus' nail-pierced hands, they recognize the Lord and their hearts glow. They recognize, experience, and embrace *God with them,* and they can't contain themselves! Their heads lift, their eyes brighten and widen, their feet lighten, their hearts are set on fire! So inspired and full to bursting are they, that in that same hour they get up and go. They don't wait until morning. They hurry back to Jerusalem to tell the great news: "The Lord has risen indeed! We have seen him! He is with us!"

The disciples experienced the power of *with.* I think that's what loving our neighbors is all about. That's what it means to be missional and incarnational.

The risen Lord showed up, not in the temple, but in cemeteries, on beaches, at home gatherings, and on the road. He ate a lot of fish and bread. Sometimes I wonder if the church has made everything too complicated. What if we all just did what Jesus did: walked alongside, listened, empathized, told the story, broke bread?

Loving our neighbors by walking with them as Jesus walks with us isn't a set of statements, structures, or monuments. It's a lifestyle. Let's manifest and participate in the tangible kingdom as God's people—actively, lovingly, and faithfully incarnating the risen Lord where we live.

Day 2

"I rejoice in your word like one who discovers a great treasure" (Ps. 119:162, English Standard Version).

Practice the Breath Prayer in a posture that is comfortable for you (see p. 16).

Then read Luke 24:13-35 and explore the following questions:

- Imagine yourself on the Emmaus road. What would you have been thinking and feeling? How would you have responded to the "stranger"? What would you have done when you found out it was Jesus?
- As you read the passage and the theme reflection, what particularly impressed you, and why?
- How would you define "incarnational"?

- Who might God be calling you to walk with in your neighborhood? How?
- What might walking with your neighbors look like? Think of a specific example.
- What will you do in response to this passage? Talk with God about what you're hearing, thinking, wrestling with, and enjoying as you seek to love your neighbors.

Pray that God will B-L-E-S-S your neighbors (see p. 33).

Day 3

"I rejoice in your word like one who discovers a great treasure" (Ps. 119:162, English Standard Version).

Practice the Breath Prayer in a posture that is comfortable for you.

Then read Isaiah 7:14, 9:6-7, and Matthew 1:21-23 and explore these questions:
- How do you experience "Immanuel"—God with us—every day? Be specific.
- Using the chart on the next page, think of at least one example from Jesus' life and ministry that demonstrates each of his titles in Isaiah. Do the same in terms of how you have experienced this character trait/ministry of Jesus. Then write down how your neighbor might experience this trait of Jesus through you.

Relax and rejoice in God's kingdom presence and rule today.

Pray that God will B-L-E-S-S your neighbors.

Titles	In Jesus' ministry	In my life	Through me to others
Wonderful Counselor			
Mighty God			
Everlasting Father			
Prince of Peace			

LIFE STORY

We had a crack house on our street for a year, with our street being used for open drug dealing. Neighbors had called the police, contacted the authorities a number of times, but to no avail. Then I began to pray for our neighborhood, including this situation. Shortly afterward, my husband (who is 6'7") came home late one evening and saw a deal going down. He got out of his van and stopped and stared at the two people. On the way into our home, he heard a loud bang but he didn't bother to check it out. The next morning we discovered that they had smashed the back van window (worth $400!).

The next day I decided to do a prayer walk. The day after that, the crack house was gone—after years of no movement! God is very gracious in answering prayers. We haven't seen any drug deals since then. And this quest to keep an eye on drug activity has brought our neighborhood together.

God continues to show me what he can do in our neighborhood. My neighbor friend and I are going to a public meeting to talk about the city's drug problems. We don't want them to just move onto someone else's street! What makes me more in awe of God is that I asked him to let me meet a neighbor lady who is my age and going through a horrible time in her life. God has allowed me to meet her twice already to really talk. —MT

Day 4

"I rejoice in your word like one who discovers a great treasure" (Ps. 119:162, English Standard Version).

Practice the Breath Prayer in a posture that is comfortable for you.

Read John 1:1-18. Take your time in the passage. Contemplate the phrases that stand out for you. Then explore these questions:

- What do you learn about the Father and the Son in this passage?
- What do you learn about "us"?
- What do you learn about the term "incarnational" from this passage?
- How does it apply to God? To Jesus' followers? What does it look like for the church to be incarnational today?

Read and think about the following quote and plan to discuss it with your group at your next meeting:

The incarnational approach to mission is refreshingly simple. It requires us to live amongst the people in our communities, love them, share the good news of the kingdom both in action and in speech and then as people become followers of Christ to form up indigenous communities of faith that reflect the specific context. This requires no great resources or buildings, no slick marketing plans and no highly talented people. ("Incarnational v. Attractional

Mission," by Andrew (Hamo) Hamilton, posted on www.backyardmissionary.com.)

Pray that God will B-L-E-S-S your neighbors.

Day 5

"I rejoice in your word like one who discovers a great treasure" (Ps. 119:162).

Practice the Breath Prayer in a posture that is comfortable for you.

Read Philippians 2:5-11, then explore the following questions:
- What stands out for you about Jesus in these verses?
- Explain this passage in your own words.
- How has (or how would) confessing "Jesus is Lord" changed your life? Your relationships? Your thought life? Your approach to work, leisure, neighbors, money?
- How does confessing "Jesus is Lord" give glory to the Father?
- Now read verses 1-5. What's the connection between Paul's urgings and the hymn of verses 6-11?

Consider verses 2-4 in the context of your neighborhood network/group life. How could/will you apply them? Think of some specific ways. Choose to do one or two of those things personally or as a group.

Pray that God will B-L-E-S-S your neighbors.

Day 6

"I rejoice in your word like one who discovers a great treasure" (Ps. 119:162, English Standard Version).

Practice the Breath Prayer in a posture that is comfortable for you.

Read Luke 24:36-49 and explore these questions:

- What strikes you about the group of people to whom Jesus appeared?
- What does it mean for you and me that Jesus' resurrection appearances happen to believing, doubting, fearful, and confused people?
- What does the passage show us/tell us about Jesus?
- When have you felt the joy and wonder (and/or the doubt and confusion) of experiencing the risen Christ? How will you share this with your neighbors today?

Pray that God will B-L-E-S-S your neighbors.

Day 7

"I rejoice in your word like one who discovers a great treasure" (Ps. 119:162, English Standard Version).

Practice the Breath Prayer in a posture that is comfortable for you.

Matthew 28:16-20 is a familiar passage often referred to as "the Great Commission." Read it, and then explore these questions:

- To whom does it apply?
- Explain in your own words what disciples are to do and what that looks like (or might look like) for you.
- What does it mean to "go"?
- To "make disciples"?
- To teach obedience to Christ's commands?
- With what assurance can we do this?
- What might the Lord want *you* to hear through this passage today?
- How will you respond to God?

You've completed Week 2! Reflect on your experience and be prepared to share it with your group tomorrow.

OUR HOME IS BIGGER THAN OUR HOUSE

Stories from the Journey

When I mentioned to my neighbor that I was going to be speaking to a group of church leaders about neighborhood life, and asked her to write down what she would say if she were me, this is one of the things she said:

> Even our dogs enjoy the life of community! Karen and I have a dog-sharing program with my Obie and her Bebe. If one of us is going to be away, the other takes the two dogs for walks during the day. All creatures are better cared for in the arms of community.

She also said that "events in our neighborhood are not anonymous now—they are connected to names, to people, to friends. . . . And, yes, day to day our lives are richer. We get to see the little ones play and grow up among us, share in tales of travel and human adventures, celebrate retirements and other events."

Another couple in our neighborhood took us out for dinner because, they said, they really appreciated what we were doing for the neighborhood. As we ate great Thai food, the conversation naturally gave us an opportunity to explain why we are so committed to our neighbors. We said things like "We believe that God wants us to love our neighbors and that when we do, everyone benefits and gets to experience a bit of the kingdom of God. We try to imagine what God would want our neighborhood to be like—a place of peace and joy and shalom."

And at some point in our conversation, one of our neighbors had an "aha" moment. For the first time, she perceived the idea that Jesus was God, and that it wasn't just that everyone could be like Jesus by being nice and good. Later she sent me a two-page email with some of her thoughts for my talk. Here is a little of what she wrote:

As I write this I know that my home is bigger than our house. We have attended several neighborhood get-togethers, and each time I am lucky enough to see my wonderful neighbors my heart is filled up with good feelings. I love having the privilege of sharing life stories with those I live near to. When I hear a part of someone's life story I feel happy and connected. I learn about myself through listening to others. When we confide in a small neighborhood gathering I gain a sense of confidence. What I mean is, I gain and grow as a person from knowing what is important to my neighbors. Good communication is a key ingredient in the evolution of neighbor into friend. For me, I would rather share a tear or a laugh than borrow a cup of sugar. I want to know the impact I have on my neighbors. If I do something that is troublesome to a family in my area, I would like the chance to fix it. If I do something that is helpful, and it bears an impact, I would like to know so that I can do more.

▤ Sideward Pursuit (Group Meeting): Teach and Counsel

"Teach and counsel each other with all the wisdom he gives" (Col. 3:16, New Living Translation).

BEING COMMUNITY

- Just for fun, consider gathering a little earlier than usual today for a potluck dinner or a hot dog and marshmallow roast around a campfire.
- Tell some stories. What's God been doing in you and in your neighborhood in response to your prayers? Make sure everyone has a chance to share.

REVIEW WEEK 2

Review and discuss each of the pursuits for Week 2. Make sure everyone has a chance to share. If your group is large, divide into smaller groups. What did you learn about yourself, about God, about your neighborhood, and about your neighbors?

⌃ **Upward:** Open Hands—Did you find this posture helpful? Why?

❮ **Inward:** Goodness—Did your understanding of goodness change at all this week?

❯ **Outward:** Praying that God will B-L-E-S-S our neighbors—Do you see your neighbors differently now that you're praying for them?

▣ DISCUSS THIS WEEK'S SIDEWARD THEME

This week our sideward pursuit instructs us to learn from each other, knowing that God works through and in each one of us. Read the following verses aloud:

> Let the message about Christ, in all its richness, fill your lives. Teach and counsel [*admonish* in most other translations] each other with all the wisdom he gives. Sing psalms and hymns and spiritual songs to God with thankful hearts. And whatever you do or say, do it as a representative of the Lord Jesus, giving thanks through him to God the Father.
>
> —Colossians 3:16-17, New Living Translation

Explore the following questions together:

- How has "the message about Christ" been filling your lives?
- How is your group being "representatives of the Lord Jesus" to one another? To your neighbors?
- What might "teaching and counseling each other with all the wisdom God gives" look like in your group?
- Invite everyone to share one thing they have learned over the last few weeks that they believe could be helpful to (teach or counsel) others.

PREPARE FOR THE PURSUITS OF THE WEEK

Review/discuss the other postures and practices for Week 3:

⬆ **Upward:** *Lectio Divina*

◀ **Inward:** Knowledge

▶ **Outward:** Making Connections

Then discuss the following questions:

- What are you feeling good about as you begin another week on the journey into neighborhood life?
- What do you want to do better in the coming week?
- How can your group support and pray for you in your efforts to "live among" your neighbors?
- How can your group support and pray for you as you engage in these postures and practices this week?

Pray together. Considering dividing by gender this week and lifting up the particular needs of the women or men in your group and neighborhoods.

Practice the following upward, inward, and outward pursuits on your own this week. Plan to complete them before your next group meeting.

⬛ Upward Pursuit: Hearing God Through His Word (Lectio Divina)

"I honor and love your commands. I meditate on your decrees" (Ps. 119:48).

By reading Scripture we can learn a lot about God, ourselves, and our mission, but often we are more motivated to "get through" the reading than to get something out of it. *Lectio divina*, the ancient tradition of meditating on Scripture handed down from Benedictine monks, can help us experience God's Word in a new way during our Time with God's Word this week. The practice of *lectio divina* has three steps:

- **Read:** Read the passage slowly and carefully two or three times. If possible, read aloud; if not, try moving your lips inaudibly as you read. Continue until you come to a verse, phrase, or word that attracts your attention or especially appeals to you.
- **Meditate:** Close your eyes and repeat your chosen phrase, verse, or word for few minutes by mouthing the words silently or saying them in your mind. Don't try to analyze the words; just let them sink in. After a while, you may want to shorten the phrase a bit. You may also want to try saying it with the emphasis on different words. As you repeat the phrase, it may help to imagine Jesus saying it directly to you.
- **Pray:** Now that you've filled your heart with God's Word, express your heartfelt feelings to God. You may want to simply

wait in silence before God, with the words in your heart. Or thank God for that particular part of his Word. Or ask God to help you live out what you have just heard him say. Or converse with God, saying whatever the phrase you chose brings to mind.

Conclude with a brief silence in which you rest in God's presence and open yourself to God's leading.

Inward Pursuit: Knowledge

"For this very reason, make every effort to add to your faith goodness; and to goodness, knowledge . . ." (2 Pet. 1:5).

In this context, knowledge refers to good judgment or good sense. Disciples seeking to be like Jesus don't do foolish things, take silly risks, or follow fools or falsehoods. Explore these questions together:

- How might your faith be supported by goodness (from Week 2) and knowledge?
- Take some mental notes (and record them later) of times when you naturally exercised good judgment/common sense and times when you tended to just jump in and throw caution (and knowledge) to the wind. Is there a time to do so? How does that fit/not fit with loving your neighbor?
- As you do your devotions and take up this week's postures and practices, ask God for knowledge, and use it.
- Share a story of a time when you did something that wasn't so smart.
- Discuss what kind of common-sense knowledge might be important for "sent" disciples to have.

Outward Pursuit: Making Connections

"Live wisely among those who are not believers, and make the most of every opportunity. Let your conversation be gracious and attractive so that you will have the right response for everyone" (Col. 4:5-6).

Here's the challenge: This week, have one or more conversations with neighbors you don't know well. A conversation is more than a wave across the street. It begins with introductions. It's time to learn people's names, what they do, how long they've been in your neighborhood, who's in their family.

The first obstacle to connecting with the reasonably friendly strangers next door is that many of us are busy—so busy that we often try to avoid making eye contact with our neighbor because we're already late for our next event. We can't imagine how we might fit in even a ten-minute chat with a "stranger."

But if we want to continue the journey toward loving our neighbors, we'll have to invest time, effort, and attention.

So take some time, effort, and attention at the beginning of this week to do a little self-assessment . . . and to make a commitment to this outward pursuit.

People (including you) have a limited number of "connectors." Overloading those connectors inhibits building and nurturing other relationships. But many of our neighbors (people in our missional contexts) have "empty" connectors.

- How full are your connectors? How full are the connectors of most people in your church? With whom are they full?
- How much space is there for new connections in your life? How will you make space?

As you think through and pray about your relationships, ask God to give you courage, conviction, and wisdom to extend yourself to others. Open up some of your connectors so you can develop sincere relationships with those in your missional context.

LIFE STORY

Isn't God so upside down? His ways are not our ways. A man who refused to ever make eye contact with me or acknowledge me was the first one to RSVP to attend our wine and cheese next weekend! Too funny. Go figure. And by the way, the response to our invitation was extremely warm. —BM

TIME WITH GOD'S WORD

Theme for the Week: Simple Is Not the Same as Easy

"'Teacher,' he asked, 'what must I do to inherit eternal life?' 'What is written in the Law?' [Jesus] replied. 'How do you read it?' He answered, '"Love the Lord your God with all your heart and with all your soul and with all your strength and with all your mind"'; and '"Love your neighbor as yourself." 'You have answered correctly,' Jesus replied. 'Do this and you will live'" (Luke 10:25-28).

"Do this and you will live"—that sounds simple enough. And it is, until you start trying to figure out how to actually *do* it.

You know what it's like. You lead a Bible study on Wednesday nights, attend choir practice on another night, bring the kids to youth group. You help out with the children's ministry and you're on a committee and you mentor a young person and you're part of a small group.

The church maintains and sustains the *status quo* very well. But perhaps you picked up this book because, despite all your maintaining and sustaining busyness, something seems to be missing. You're tired. You're bored with playing it safe, with keeping life clean and well-vacuumed. You're looking for an investment that will have greater returns.

If God is a sending God and we are his sent ones filled and empowered by his Spirit, there must be more to being sent than supporting missionaries overseas and having an outreach committee at church. Being missional must actually be about acknowledging that we are *all* missionaries—right where we are. Every believer is a church planter, as Alan Hirsch proclaims.

So what would it look like to invest our lives—your life—in pursuit of the call to get out of the pew and out of the cocoon of safety that we've spun for ourselves?

Perhaps this isn't about adding more activities to already-full schedules. Perhaps "more" is actually *less*. Be who you're called and made to be—the presence of Jesus where you are, in your own back and front yard, loving God and neighbor. That's the call and design of the missional God. Sounds simple, right?

Yes. But simple is not the same as easy.

Day 2

"The unfolding of your words gives light; it gives understanding to the simple" (Ps. 119:130).

Practice the Breath Prayer in a posture that is comfortable for you.

> "A missional theology is not content with mission being a church-based work. Rather, it applies to the whole life of every believer. Every disciple is to be an agent of the kingdom of God, and every disciple is to carry the mission of God into every sphere of life. . . . Missional represents a significant shift in the way we think about the church. As the people of a missionary God, we ought to engage the world the same way he does—by going out rather than just reaching out."

("Defining Missional," © Alan Hirsch, reprinted by permission from *Leadership Journal*. www.leadershipjournal.net)

Read Luke 19:11-27, *lectio divina* style (see p. 45). Then explore the following questions:

- As you read the passage and the theme reflection, what might God want you to hear?
- What challenged you? Why?
- What convicted you? Why?
- What encouraged or comforted you? Why?
- How will you respond?
- Talk with God about what you're hearing, thinking, wrestling with, and enjoying during this study.

Day 3

"The unfolding of your words gives light; it gives understanding to the simple" (Ps. 119:130).

Practice the Breath Prayer in a posture that is comfortable for you.

Read Mark 1:16-20 and 2:13-14, *lectio divina* style. Then explore the following questions:
- Imagine yourself going about your daily work when a young, relatively unknown teacher comes by and asks you to "come and follow" him. How do you respond? What goes through your mind?
- What motivated those first disciples to drop everything and follow? What did following Jesus entail for them?
- What does following Jesus entail for you?
- What might God be asking you to "drop" in order to follow him today? Where might Jesus be leading you?
- Select a verse or phrase to "chew on" as you go about your life today.

This week, remember to be praying for your neighbors and intentionally pursuing opportunities to connect.

Day 4

"The unfolding of your words gives light; it gives understanding to the simple" (Ps. 119:130).

Practice the Breath Prayer in a posture that is comfortable for you.

Read and meditate on Matthew 22:34-40, *lectio divina* style. Then explore the following questions:
- How do these two commandments summarize the entire law and the commands of the prophets (or the Ten Commandments)?

- How are you keeping these two commandments? Be honest with yourself. If you had to score yourself from one to ten, what score would you get?
- What could you do this week to increase your score? What will you do?
- Could following Jesus really come down to just loving God and loving our neighbor? Isn't it a lot more complicated than that? Has the church made it too complicated through the centuries? If so, how? Why do we struggle with going back to the basics?
- If you (re)committed yourself to keeping these two commandments faithfully, intentionally, and consistently, how would that change you (your lifestyle, relationships, activities, attitude, choices)?
- If your group (re)committed to keeping these two commandments, faithfully, intentionally, consistently, what impact would that have?

This week, remember to be praying for your neighbors and intentionally pursuing opportunities to connect.

Day 5

"The unfolding of your words gives light; it gives understanding to the simple" (Ps. 119:130).

Practice the Breath Prayer in a posture that is comfortable for you.

Read and meditate on Matthew 5:13-16, *lectio divina* style. Then explore the following questions:
- What are you? What do you do?
- How can you flavor your neighborhood? How can we together flavor our neighborhood?
- How can you give light to your neighborhood? How can we together give light to our neighborhood?

- What good deeds will you do in your neighborhood that will "shine before others, that they may . . . glorify your Father in heaven" (v. 16)?

Share some ways you sprinkled some salt in your neighborhood this week.

Commit to doing one good deed (however small) in your neighborhood this week.

Pray that your group will expand its salt and light impact. Pray that God's kingdom will come and God's will be done on your street (on earth) as it is in heaven.

Day 6

"The unfolding of your words gives light; it gives understanding to the simple" (Ps. 119:130).

Practice the Breath Prayer in a posture that is comfortable for you.

Read and meditate on Matthew 17:20-21 and 21:21-22, *lectio divina* style. Then explore the following questions:
- Sometimes we excuse ourselves from acting on what we believe with thoughts like, "I need more faith" or "If I only knew more about the Bible." How do these verses from Matthew challenge that kind of thinking?
- Describe the God you have faith in. What is this God like?
- What will you pray for with your "mustard seed" faith today? What mountain needs to be moved in your life? In your neighborhood?

Thank God for your faith, and pray with the father of the demon-possessed boy, "I do believe; help me overcome my unbelief!" (Mark 9:24).

Day 7

"The unfolding of your words gives light; it gives understanding to the simple" (Ps. 119:130).

Practice the Breath Prayer in a posture that is comfortable for you.

Read and meditate on Isaiah 6:1-9, *lectio divina* style. Then explore the following questions:

- Imagine yourself in the presence of God (after all, you *are* there!). At what times in your life have you been struck by the glory and holiness of the Lord? How did you respond?
- What leads Isaiah (and us) to an awareness of our "uncleanness"? Why might that awareness be important?
- How or when have you experienced God removing your guilt and forgiving your sins?

Don't play it safe; respond in prayer to God as Isaiah did, saying "Here I am, Lord, send me."

As Isaiah was sent to a certain people, so are you. Who do you think God might be sending you to?

LIFE STORY

PK had given me the booklet *Praying the Lord's Prayer for Your Neighbors*. It sounded like a good, safe way to express God's love for my neighbors without actually having to come in contact with them. No messy conversations or awkward social exchanges and all the glory of being able to check that duty off my list—*until all those prayers started to be answered.*

A retired couple, our neighbors, came to us about replacing the fence between our houses. That led to being invited into their home for the first time for tea as well as initiating conversations with the rest of our fence neighbors, some of whom we had never met after living there for three years. Turns out one is even an Olympic gold medalist—in fencing!

When the fence contractor proved incompetent, the retired couple were beside themselves. What to do with a fence that's half built, paid for, and leaning in two different directions? We settled the business deal for them and called in the troops. On the first day, our extended family came over, tore down the worst of it, and rebuilt the back section. A few days later, a team from our church's CIA (Community In Action) arrived to finish another few sections.

Our neighbors were astonished. They couldn't believe the kindness of our friends. When I told them that we were just getting to know them ourselves and that this is a ministry of our church, they said, "Lovely, just lovely. Now that's the kind of church I could be a part of!"

So the fence saga continues. We have yet to start the other sides of our fence and there are still four sections to finish on the retired couple's fence, but the ground has been broken for future relationships. Last week a man from across the street stopped by while walking his dog and offered to help us finish it. Someone we had never met before! Who knows what else might happen as we continue to pray and meet our neighbors over the fence?—JJ

THE CITY GETS IT

Stories from the Journey

A group of pastors representing twenty churches in a large city gathered to think and dream about this question: How could their congregations come together to serve their community? They invited the mayor to talk about his dream for their city and the issues that he felt were preventing that dream from becoming a reality.

The mayor came with a list of pervasive issues and problems, including at-risk kids, elderly homebound people, dilapidated housing, hunger. But before delving into these issues, he said, "The majority of the problems that our community is facing would be eliminated or drastically reduced if we could just become a community of people who are great neighbors."

The value the mayor gave to neighboring resonated with many others in the room. As one pastor put it, "Here we were asking the mayor what areas of the city were most in need, and he basically told us that it would be great if we could just get our people to obey the second half of the Great Commandment."

The assistant city manager also spoke, but among other things he noted that "from the city's perspective, there isn't a noticeable difference in how Christians and non-Christians 'neighbor' in our community."

Maybe it's time there *is* a difference. Maybe those who seek to follow Jesus should be the initiators—the community menders and makers in neighborhoods across the continent. The "powers that be" certainly see the value of it, so shouldn't we?

Jim Diers (see www.neighborpower.org), who has worked on neighborhood empowerment projects around the globe for years, is serving my city as a consultant. As a result, Edmonton has now invested in and is committed to a Great Neighborhoods initiative. A first step was an invitation to residents to host "Front Room Forums" with their neighbors to discuss what would make our communities even better places to live.

My husband and I invited everyone we knew in the neighborhood to come to our house, enjoy dessert and coffee, and discuss our city. It was fascinating! We learned a lot about differing views over our little municipal airport, about drug deals happening in our back alleys (that was a shock!), and about what was important to our neighbors. It was an enlightening evening, and we got to know a few neighbors we had barely met before.

Next the city encouraged neighbors to gather and dream about their particular community and to submit applications for local projects they would like to implement. We did that too, and had another great evening . . . and guess what we came up with?

- More opportunities for people to connect—how about monthly potlucks at the Community Hall (sounds a lot like what the church often calls "fellowship").

- Good Neighbors Days—days when people could volunteer to help elderly or single-parent households, clean up the parks, and so on (sounds a lot like diaconal work to me).
- There was great enthusiasm for a bigger project: taking over an abandoned house and lot that the city owns and making it into a coffeehouse where neighborhood groups could meet, local artists could show their work, people could just hang out—and all profits could go back into the community.

What if the church really moved into the neighborhood, partnering with and living among those with whom we're planted?

Our neighborhood proposal was one of fifteen chosen, and we were invited to participate in a day-long workshop with Jim Diers. It was inspiring! And now we have the opportunity to make these dreams and goals a reality. Many neighbors are engaged, and the city councillor and other city support staff are on board. The amazing thing is that they are all keeping the "second greatest commandment," and they may not even know it!

As one neighbor put it, "The projects aren't really the goal. The goal is to build community, to develop more and better connections among neighbors." Wow, the kingdom of God is near!

"Seek the peace and prosperity of the city to which I have carried you into exile. Pray to the LORD for it, because if it prospers, you too will prosper" (Jer. 29:7).

WEEK 4 PURSUITS ⬒ ⬑ ◀ ▶

⬒ Sideward Pursuit (Group Meeting): Do Good to All

BEING COMMUNITY
- Enjoy a potluck dessert buffet or other refreshments.
- Share a story about or describe the neighborhood in which you grew up.

Review Week 3

Review and discuss the postures and practices of Week 3:

⬒ **Sideward:** Teach and Counsel—What did you learn this week from someone else in your group or neighborhood?

⬑ **Upward:** *Lectio divina*—How was this different than studying for information? Share a verse or two that stood out for you (which ones did you meditate on?), and explain why.

◀ **Inward:** Knowledge—Share a story or two about when you did or didn't exercise common sense. The "didn't" stories are fun for all to hear—don't worry, your group will be laughing with you, not at you!

▶ **Outward:** Making Connections—How did God open doors and conversations for you? How are you making room for your neighbors?

Ask yourselves these general questions:
- What went well in your efforts to love your neighbors this past week?
- What are you "shoulding" yourself about?

- What do you want to do different or better this week? How will you do it?

☑ DISCUSS THIS WEEK'S SIDEWARD THEME

This week's theme is inclusiveness. Who in your neighborhood might feel left out or on the fringes? How might being more inclusive be another way to quit "playing it safe"?

Consider these three "B-words": Behave, Belong, Believe. These are three ways of measuring how people are included in a community. Explore the following questions together:

- Share in what order you have experienced the three "B-words" in your church community. Discuss how churches tend to expect these words to be ordered when enfolding newcomers.
- Which "B-word" do you think came first in Jesus' life and message? Share some examples.
- What do these words have to do with making others feel included and accepted in your neighborhood?
- How have you, your group, and your church tended to live these words out?
- How do you *want* to live them out? How will you do that?

> "Evangelism is about helping people belong so that they come to believe. Most people today do not 'decide' to believe. In community, they 'discover' that they believe, and then they decide to affirm that publicly and to follow Christ intentionally. People are looking for a safe, accepting place to develop their identity and sense of self in community."
>
> (Rick Richardson, *Evangelism Outside the Box*, 2000, p. 100)

PREPARE FOR THE PURSUITS OF THE WEEK

Review and discuss the other postures and practices for Week 4:

🔼 **Upward:** Praying A-C-T-S

◀ **Inward:** Self-Control

▶ **Outward:** Including and doing good to all. Read the passage and discuss the questions related to this pursuit together as a group. Make plans to host Matthew Parties and do good in your neighborhood(s) in the next few weeks. (If you all live in different neighborhoods, it may not be possible to have a party in every neighborhood in one week!)

Entertain any other thoughts or comments about the theme reflection and Time with God's Word.

Close with prayer. You might want to try praying the Lord's Prayer together for yourselves and your neighbors. Ask one person to lead with a phrase from the prayer, and leave time for others to make petitions that follow that phrase's theme. For example:

> **Our Father . . .**
> Thank you for being our Father. Thank you that you know us, love us, and accept us just as we are. Be a Father to J and M. Help S, T, and V to know you as their Father.

Practice the following upward, inward, and outward pursuits on your own this week. Plan to complete them before your next group meeting.

Upward Pursuit: **Praying A-C-T-S**

"Devote yourselves to prayer, being watchful and thankful. And pray for us, too. . ." (Col. 4:2-3)

Prayer is our conversation with God. As in any relationship, good communication is central, foundational, and multifaceted. If, for example, all we do is ask someone for things or tell them what to do, they aren't going to want to hang out with us too often! In a healthy relationship, we say "Thank you," "I'm sorry," and "I love you," along with the "could you please-es." The same is true in our relationship with God, yet it is so easy to get in the habit of just being an asker. This week, we'll work on our conversation skills using the acronym A-C-T-S. (There's a second "s," but we'll save that for another week.) During your devotional time, complete the sentence under each heading for your prayer. Write the responses if you wish.

"A" is for Adoration

We praise the people we know and love by saying things like "You look great tonight, honey!" "John, you're so good at helping people!" or "Marta, you're such an encourager!" We can and should praise and adore the God whom we know and love. Check out these verses to see some examples: Exodus 15:2; Isaiah 25:1; Psalm 33; 71:16; 99:1-5; 135:3.

I adore and praise you, Lord, for your . . .

_____

_____

"C" is for Confession

Sometimes we make mistakes, say the wrong thing, forget, or mess up, and we need to apologize and seek forgiveness to make things right again. This is also true when we pause and think through our day from God's perspective: what we thought, said, and did, as well as what we didn't think, say, or do. This exercise might be a little unsettling if you haven't done it before. But, thanks be to God, when we repent (confess and turn from our sin), God forgives, forgets, and embraces us in his big arms of grace. Check out Psalm 32:5; Psalm 51:17; 1 John 1:8-9.

Lord, I confess . . .

_____

_____

"T" is for Thanksgiving

When we were small we learned to say "thank you," and that should be a lifelong practice! Start a list of things to thank God for, and add to it all week. Read Psalm 52:9; 107:8; Matthew 11:25; Philippians 1:3.

I thank you, Lord . . .

"S" is for Supplication

Supplication is the act of asking God for the things we and others need. Continue to pray for your neighbors—the people in your missional context with whom you are developing relationships. Pray also that your neighborhood would be inclusive. Pray for family, friends, the church, your work, the city, the formation of neighborhoods across the nation. Pray for peace, justice, equity around the world . . . there is no end of things to pray for! Check out 1 Samuel 12:23; Psalm 122:6; Matthew 5:44; 2 Thessalonians 1:11; 3:1.

Lord, I ask for others . . .

Lord, I ask for myself . . .

Inward Pursuit: Self-Control

"For this very reason, make every effort to add to your faith goodness; and to goodness, knowledge; and to knowledge, self-control . . ." (2 Pet. 1:5-6).

- What is self-control?
- How does it complement goodness and knowledge?
- How well do you exercise self-control in frustrating circumstances? In the face of temptation?
- How might having (or not having) self-control impact us as "participants in the divine nature" (v. 4) who want to be effective and fruitful (v. 8)?
- When or how might self-control be important as you and your group seek to be more inclusive?
- If you dare, keep track of your efforts at self-control this week and talk with God about them.

To learn more about this character trait, check out Proverbs 5:23; 16:32; 25:28; Galatians 5:23; 1 Peter 1:13; 2 Timothy 3:1-5.

▶ Outward Pursuit: The Matthew Party

Your outward pursuit this week is to plan, schedule, and prepare for a "Matthew Party." Read the following Scripture passage, and discuss the questions below.

"As Jesus was walking along, he saw a man named Matthew sitting at his tax collector's booth. 'Follow me and be my disciple,' Jesus said to him. So Matthew got up and followed him. Later, Matthew invited Jesus and his disciples to his home as dinner guests, along with many tax collectors and other disreputable sinners. But when the Pharisees saw this, they asked his disciples, 'Why does your teacher eat with such scum?' When Jesus heard this, he said, 'Healthy people don't need a doctor— sick people do.' Then he added, 'Now go and learn the meaning of this Scripture: "I want you to show mercy, not offer sacrifices." For I have come to call not those who think they are righteous, but those who know they are sinners.'" (Matt. 9:9-13, New Living Translation)

- What's happening in this story?
- According to what you read, what might a Matthew Party look like? Who participates?

- What neighbors and disciples might you bring together? How?

A Matthew Party is a social gathering modeled after Matthew 9:9-13. The concept is to invite your Christ-following friends and your other friends and neighbors together for a party (and let God do the rest!).

Plan Matthew Parties for the neighborhoods in which you live. Consider . . . .

- Whom will you invite and how?
- When and where it will be?
- What will you serve?
- What activities will you plan?

Matthew Party Suggestions

Backyard Barbecue

Bridge for Fun: learn the game together over wine and munchies

Campfire

Dessert and Coffee

International Dinner: everyone brings a dish from their ethnic background

Outdoor Movie Night: show a family-friendly film on the garage door. One suggestion: "Because of Winn-Dixie."

Progressive Potluck: serve each course in a different home on your street

Red Party: red food, red clothes, red drinks

Spectator Nights: watch the Super Bowl, Stanley Cup, or Academy Awards together

Theme Tea Parties: Victorian, Mad Hatter

Theme Meals: fondue, sushi, grill

Wine, Cheese, and Art Night

Weekend Brunch or Pancake Breakfast

Yard Games Night: Bocce, croquet, bean bag toss, and more

TIME WITH GOD'S WORD

Theme for the Week: No Undesirables

In Jesus' day, the religious leaders had taken God's guidelines for his people and turned them into black-and-white "you're in, you're not" labels. To be "in," you had to be righteous and undefiled—which meant you had to obey the leaders' interpretations of the 613 commandments they had found in the Bible. You had to wear your clothes, do your hair, listen to music, pray, eat your lunch, and wash your hands *their way*—or else you were OUT! It was as if the leaders had put up a sign reading **"No Undesirables Allowed!"**

There is nothing wrong with defining who we are, but there is something terribly wrong with condemning others as undesirable, undeserving, unworthy, unclean!

Jesus' followers needed some help learning this lesson. They had lived with labels all their lives, so much so that divine intervention was required for them to remove the labels and discover that other people, not just Jews, were made in God's image and loved by God. That was a revelation! It was such a revelation, such a new thing, that Luke spends sixty-six verses describing it and repeats the essence of the story three times in Acts 10 and 11.

God wants to include the Gentiles among his people. And when God wants to do something, it gets done. So God sends a vision to a man named Cornelius, a "man who feared God with all his household," but to Jews, even Jesus' disciples, he was an outsider.

Peter also receives a vision from God of an "unholy" mixture of clean and unclean animals let down from heaven in a sheet. In Peter's day, Jews did not want to come in contact with anything unclean—whether food or people—because they believed it would defile them. But God has different ideas. God says, "Take off your labels, Peter!" But it's such a paradigm shift for Peter that he continues to puzzle over it. So God disrupts Peter's puzzlement with a clear command:

> Then a voice told him, "Get up, Peter. Kill and eat." "Surely not, Lord!" Peter replied. "I have never eaten anything impure or unclean." The voice spoke to him a second time, "Do not call anything impure that God has made clean" (Acts 10:13-15).

Who have we "churched people" labeled unclean? Pause and ask yourself "Who have *I* labeled?" Be honest—who do you avoid? Maybe it's people who are unemployed, homosexual, from other countries, divorced. . . .

Hear the Lord speak the truth in love to you: "What God has made clean you must not call impure. In my kingdom there are no undesirables. Jesus died once for all."

Peter didn't have very long to let his vision sink in. While he was still wondering what the vision meant, Cornelius's representatives came knocking at his door to ask him to come to Cornelius's house. And he did. Peter, the Jew, got up and went to the house of a Gentile! While he was there, Luke tells us, this Gentile "outsider" believed and was baptized, together with his whole family, as the Holy Spirit came upon them.

This is huge. This story isn't just about the conversion of Cornelius—this story is about the conversion of Peter's heart. Often, Christians are the biggest barrier to the spreading and receiving of the Good News. Those who think they are clean, those who claim to be insiders—sometimes they're the ones who need a conversion.

There are no "undesirables" in the kingdom of God! Can we get that through our heads? We know that God loves everyone. Some of us have been hearing that since we were in our mother's womb. But do we live it?

Perhaps we need to start over again. Perhaps we need to go to Cornelius's house rather than expecting Cornelius to come to us and become like us.

It was God's vision, God's mission, to include the Gentiles with the Jews. God was the director, instigator, mover, shaker, eye-opener—and he still is. Because God is working in us *and* in our neighbors, we don't have to have it all figured out. We do, however, have to be attentive to the Spirit and realize that God isn't just changing our neighbor, but us too.

Day 2

"Make them holy by your truth; teach them your word, which is truth" (John 17:17, New Living Translation).

Practice the Breath Prayer in a posture that is comfortable for you.

Read Acts 10, *lectio divina* style. Then explore these questions:
- What inspired, amazed, or surprised you about this story?
- What made you squirm?
- Note the work of the Holy Spirit throughout the account.
- How is this story a call for Peter and all believers to be inclusive?
- How will you respond?

Pray through your thoughts and feelings using A-C-T-S (see p. 60).
- How inclusive is your missional community/neighborhood network? Is there anyone you've been excluding?
- How will you extend welcome, grace, and inclusivity this week?

Day 3

"Make them holy by your truth; teach them your word, which is truth" (John 17:17, New Living Translation).

Practice the Breath Prayer in a posture that is comfortable for you.

Read and meditate on Ephesians 2:11-22, *lectio divina* style. Then explore the following questions:

- What does this passage tell us about God's people? (List at least five things.)
- What light does it shed on this week's theme: "No Undesirables"?
- Think about (and describe to your group) a time when you felt like an outsider (v. 11) and/or were excluded (v. 12). How do these verses add to your understanding of the theme passage and reflections?
- What are the implications of the church/your missional community/neighborhood network/home group being God's house (v. 20), a holy temple (v. 21)? Be specific.
- How could you ensure that through him *all* are being made part of this dwelling where God lives by his Spirit (v. 22)?

Pray the A-C-T-S prayer.

Day 4

"Make them holy by your truth; teach them your word, which is truth" (John 17:17, New Living Translation).

Practice the Breath Prayer in a posture that is comfortable for you.

Read and meditate on Acts 2:42-47, *lectio divina* style. Then explore the following questions:
- What stands out for you in this passage?
- Note the four movements (Upward, Sideward, Inward, Outward) in these verses. How does this description reflect or not reflect your current experience?
- Keeping in mind that this passage is descriptive, not prescriptive, how could you "regroup" to be more of an Acts 2 community? What would be your first priority?
- What will you personally do in response to this passage?
- What will your missional community/neighborhood network do?

Pray A-C-T-S with your neighbors in mind.

Day 5

"Make them holy by your truth; teach them your word, which is truth" (John 17:17, New Living Translation).

Practice the Breath Prayer in a posture that is comfortable for you.

Read and meditate on Acts 18:7-11, *lectio divina* style. Then explore the following questions:
- Where does Paul stay? For how long?
- What impact do Paul's presence and message have?
- How might you claim the Lord's words to Paul as the Lord's words to you? To your neighborhood network? What will you do with this assurance and encouragement?

Pray for all the people in your city who belong to the Lord, especially for those in your missional community/neighborhood network.

Day 6

"Make them holy by your truth; teach them your word, which is truth" (John 17:17, New Living Translation).

Practice the Breath Prayer in a posture that is comfortable for you.

Read and meditate on John 17:20-26, *lectio divina* style. Then explore the following questions:
- What do we learn about the relationship between Father and Son in these verses?
- What is Jesus' prayer for his followers?
- In your opinion, how is the church doing at reflecting "one-ness," or "perfect unity" (v. 23)?
- What impact, according to this passage, might being "one" have on the world (or your neighborhood) in knowing Jesus?
- How could you work toward greater oneness and unity among believers in your neighborhood?

Talk with Jesus about his prayer for his followers. You may want to use verses 11-19 to shape your part of the conversation. Pray also for other believers in your neighborhood, that you might connect with them and that they might be open and eager to join in the journey *together*.

Day 7

"Make them holy by your truth; teach them your word, which is truth" (John 17:17, New Living Translation).

Practice the Breath Prayer in a posture that is comfortable for you.

Read and meditate on Romans 12:4-6, *lectio divina* style. Then explore the following questions:

- How are followers of Jesus like a human body?
- What body part are you most like? What parts do members of your group remind you of? (Share with each other.)
- What do Jesus' instructions challenge us to do and not to do?
- How does this comparison enrich your understanding of what it means to embrace others and do good to all?

Pray the A-C-T-S prayer with the body of Christ as your theme.

LIFE STORY

For 17 years we lived mostly on the cul-de-sac side of our house and we didn't see many people going by. We put an addition on our home with a strong sense that God wanted to use it for his kingdom.

Now, with our brand-new addition, we live on the main street side, since our garage entrance is there. It has changed our whole perspective on our neighborhood. We want to start reaching out more, and now the doors of opportunity seem to be opening more and more. —LF

CAN YOU COME FOR DINNER?

Stories from the Journey

Having meals with the strangers from your neighborhood might seem rather intimidating at first. We can come up with a lot of "what if's" that might cause us to hesitate: What if they don't like what I prepare? What if their kid has allergies? What if their religious laws forbid them from eating something? What if we don't know what to say? What if they stay too long?

Inviting strangers over can be scary, but sharing a meal really is one of the primary ways we move from being acquaintances to being in relationship. The church community gets this. Congregations are usually quite good at having regular potlucks or other events where a meal is served. So why does it seem like such a stretch for us to move beyond the boundaries of the building to embrace the people next door? I don't know why this is hard. But I do know that once we do it, life is fuller and richer (and we may end up not having to cook so often)!

We've made a commitment to eat with neighbors at least once a week. Once a month, everyone in our neighborhood is invited to a community social—a Matthew Party. On the other weeks, we have neighbors over for a meal at our house or we eat a meal at theirs. A couple of weeks ago, a neighbor called and said she had bought a big ham because she felt like it, but her kids didn't really like ham—so would we like to come for dinner? "Sure!" I replied, "and I'll bring potatoes and salad." Another time, we had leftover chili (a lot of it) so we called the couple across the street to see if they would like to join us for supper.

No matter what food is on the table, the things that go on around the table are the real blessing. For example, when families come to our house they know that we pray before we eat, so we've ended up praying with neighbors who might not usually pray together.

WEEK 5 PURSUITS ▣ ▣ ▣ ▣

▣ Sideward Pursuit (Group Meeting): Love One Another

BEING COMMUNITY

"Dear friends, let us love one another, for love comes from God" (1 John 4:7).

- Have a cheese-tasting, or share other appetizers together.
- Share good and bad experiences of getting together with people you didn't know well.

REVIEW WEEK 4
Review and discuss the postures and practices of Week 4:

▣ **Sideward:** How did the challenge of inclusivity and "doing good to all" show up during your week?

▣ **Upward:** How did using the A-C-T-S model impact your prayer time? What did you discover about your relationship with God?

▣ **Inward:** Self-Control—How did you exercise or not exercise self-control this week?

▣ **Outward:** Matthew Party—Review your plans and/or share stories about your neighborhood parties.

What stood out for you in this week's Time with God's Word?

▣ Discuss This Week's Sideward Theme
- What might loving one another have to do with loving our neighbor?

- What does loving one another have to do with loving God?
- The command to love one another is repeated numerous times in the Bible. Why do you think this is so?
- Why might loving one another in your neighborhood be important for the kingdom?

LIFE STORY

Our "wine and cheese" gathering went really well. People started arriving at 7:00, and we had about seventeen adults and three children grace our house. People were so appreciative of having the chance to get together. God's grace was so apparent. Some couples stayed until around 10:30 p.m.! Now we can pray by name for our neighbors.

I even phoned one of our younger neighbors on Sunday asking for help to put a baby seat in the car correctly—quite out of character for me as normally I find it quite difficult to ask for help! (Oh, the shame of pride, but God is working on me!) It gave us another opportunity to connect with this young family.

One of our neighbors, who could not make it to the "wine and cheese" because of his wife's migraine, stopped and talked to me on Monday and say that perhaps we could get together and have a coffee or something, so we will be following up with them!

We are hoping that this is just the beginning. We will connect individually with some and then perhaps have an afternoon barbecue or something else in a month or so. It certainly makes us more aware and, hopefully, more mindful of those around us.
—HM

PREPARE FOR THE PURSUITS OF THE WEEK
Review and discuss the other postures and practices for Week 5.
Upward: Heart Prayers
Inward: Perseverance
Outward: Refrigerator Rights

Pray for one another. Don't forget to pray for your Matthew Parties, relationship building, and neighbors too!

"Dear brothers and sisters, we can't help but thank God for you, because your faith is flourishing and your love for one another is growing" (2 Thess. 1:3).

Practice the following upward, inward, and outward pursuits on your own this week. Plan to complete them before your next group meeting.

Upward Pursuit: **Heart Prayers**

"Lord Jesus Christ, have mercy on me" (Luke 18:35-43).

One long-standing Christian tradition encourages us to pray the words, "Lord Jesus Christ, have mercy on me" as often as possible during the day. Some people pray it hundreds or thousands of times. While some Christ-followers find this prayer very helpful for "constant prayer," many of us find it more meaningful to write our own prayer in a short phrase that sums up the desire of our heart.

Try writing a "heart prayer." Your prayer should have no more than ten syllables, and it should include an address such as "God, Jesus, Father, Lord, King of Kings, Redeemer, Savior, Prince of Peace, Perfect Friend." It should also express a deeply felt desire or conviction that is on your mind and in your heart at this time. Here are some examples:

- Lord, help me to be more like you.
- Savior, may I love as you love.
- Prince of Peace, make me a person of peace.
- God, give me the courage to live for you.

Words from Scripture such as those that have caught your attention as you have practiced *lectio divina* also make good heart prayers. Consider Psalm 19:14; 26:2; 28:7; 51:10, 15; 61:2; 119:36; 139:23.

Write your heart prayer here:

_____

_____

_____

_____

Now close your eyes, relax, and pray your heart prayer for two or three minutes. Concentrate on a different key word each time, and think about what it means as you pray. Try to visualize your prayer moving from your head to your heart. Try phrasing it musically or rhythmically. Try saying it in unison with your breathing. Hold it close to your heart all week.

◀ Inward Pursuit: **Perseverance**

"For this very reason, make every effort to add to your faith goodness; and to goodness, knowledge; and to knowledge, self-control; and to self-control, perseverance . . ." (2 Pet. 1:5, 6).

It's Week 5; we're past the halfway point. How's it going? Are you growing personally, communally, missionally? Are you persevering in your commitment to love your neighbors?

Think about these questions:

- What does perseverance mean to you? What do you think it means in the Bible?
- Why might followers of Jesus need to be able to persevere in order to truly love their neighbors and engage in their neighborhoods?
- What's the connection between faith and perseverance (check out James 1:3-4).
- What else do you learn about perseverance (and character) from Romans 5:3-4?

Pray the following prayer adapted from Colossians 1:11-12. Change the personal pronouns first for yourself and then for each person in your group/network:

> I pray that [I, Jill, Miguel] will be strengthened with all God's glorious power so [I, Jill, Miguel] will have all the perseverance and patience [I, Jill, Miguel] need[s]. May [I, Jill, Miguel] always be filled with joy and always thank God.

▶ Outward Pursuit: Refrigerator Rights

"Let mutual love continue. Do not neglect to show hospitality to strangers, for by doing that some have entertained angels without knowing it" (Heb. 13:1-2).

Hospitality is central to God's intentions for extending his grace and kingdom. Will Miller and Glenn Sparks, in their book *Refrigerator Rights: Creating Connections and Restoring Relationships*, talk about how the loss of community is related to so many emotional and social ills. They suggest that it's not that people don't know a lot of people, it's that the quality of most relationships is so shallow.

People who do not know their neighbor families have no way of knowing that there is harm underway. It's not about spying; it's about having relationships with the people around us. The parent whose stress level gets so high that they take it out on their spouse or children has no one in their life to catch the signs early and ward off the tragedy. It isn't rocket science. It's about block parties, neighborhood meetings and organizing gatherings for the families and children on your street. Cookouts, gourmet clubs, touch football games are easy sells and the bonding that takes place is the beginning of cohesion and community health. These are all "Refrigerator Rights" issues.

(Dr. Will Miller, posted 11/3/2006 on fridgerights.blogspot.com)

They recommend restoring "refrigerator rights"; in other words, getting to know others well enough that you and they feel comfortable enough to get a snack from the other person's fridge.

With how many people do you have mutual refrigerator rights? Share your experiences with your group.

TIME WITH GOD'S WORD

Theme for the Week: Eating Together Is a Kingdom Activity

"So whether you eat or drink or whatever you do, do it all for the glory of God" (1 Cor. 10:31).

The Bible pictures God's kingdom as a feast (Isa. 25:6; Rev. 19:7). That tells me that there is much more to eating a meal with my neighbors than filling our stomachs.

Perhaps making macaroni is not a mundane activity. Perhaps offering people "refrigerator rights" has more to do with relationship than with hunger. Perhaps eating together actually means something, does something, restores and renews something beyond our need for physical nourishment.

I have experienced the importance of sharing a meal with people, and I am sure you have too. It often happens when the whole extended family manages to get together for a big family meal on a special occasion: Thanksgiving, Christmas, Easter, a birthday, or an anniversary. You look around and realize how much you love the people in that room. There's a profound sense of being a family—of being together.

But I have had other experiences beyond our extended family gatherings that made eating with people even more important to me. When we invited our neighbors to join us for Thanksgiving dinner, we shared family traditions and enjoyed each other's food, heard their stories, and laughed and talked and ate together late into the evening. It was a memorable meal, and my kids still talk about the old uncle of one neighbor who joined us.

When we sit down and eat together, when we invite people to share a meal with us, we communicate several things: You're welcome here. We trust you and we consider you one of us—you belong, you're accepted, you're welcome. Sharing a meal says, in a nonverbal way, "We are family."

Eating together pushes the "pause" button. When we gather around a meal, we slow down long enough to talk about more than the weather. It's an opportunity to really listen and really be heard, to relax and be present with one another.

Eating together makes it possible for us both to give and receive. Usually our guests want to bring something to the meal, and this enriches the connection. It becomes *our* meal that we're enjoying together. Even the cleaning up can be a communal time!

Eating together evokes a natural "eucharistic" response. Recognize that word? In the early Church, communion was often called the "Eucharist," meaning "giving of thanks." In other words, by the time we're sipping our coffee together and savoring our dessert, we're feeling thankful, content—for the food and the company.

Church people often joke that there's always plenty of food available at church gatherings. It's not just because we like to eat (which we do!)—it's because we thrive on table fellowship with others and with Jesus. It meets our need for community, and true community is at the heart of kingdom culture and gospel grace.

What if welcoming others to the table is a way of introducing them to the kingdom? And what if, when we invite neighbors and in the presence of the King eat together, the kingdom comes?

Day 2

" . . . so that all God's people may be thoroughly equipped for every good work" (2 Tim. 3:17).

Practice the Breath Prayer and/or your Heart Prayer in a posture that's comfortable for you.

Read Luke 14:15-24, *lectio divina* style. Then explore the following questions:

- Imagine yourself as a guest and then imagine yourself as the servant. Who might God want you to invite to his banquet?
- Read, highlight, and ponder the theme reflection. What stood out for you? Why?
- Summarize this week's theme in your own words.

Pause and ponder a Heart Prayer response and then pray it all day.

Day 3

" . . . so that all God's people may be thoroughly equipped for every good work" (2 Tim. 3:17).

Practice the Breath Prayer and/or your Heart Prayer in a posture that's comfortable for you.

Read and meditate on Luke 19:5-10, *lectio divina* style. Then explore these questions:
- What social boundaries were crossed in this story?
- What social boundaries might we need to cross as we invite neighbors to eat with us?
- How did having a meal with Jesus impact Zacchaeus?
- How has or how might having a meal (or two) with you impact your neighbors?

"When you sit down to a meal, your primary concern should not be to feed your own face but to share the life of Jesus. So be sensitive and courteous to the others who are eating. Don't eat or say or do things that might interfere with the free exchange of love" (Rom. 14:21, *The Message*).

Remember to pray your Heart Prayer regularly.

"A primary place for spiritual formation, formation-by-resurrection, is the daily meals we sit down to in the course of our daily work. Every time we pick up a knife and fork, every time we say, 'pass the salt, please,' every time we take a second helping of cauliflower, we are in a setting congenial to spiritual formation. Luke and John are telling us to take meal times seriously. Our Sunday worship is important. The Bible studies we attend are important. The retreats we make are important. But over a lifetime, the unnoticed and unrecognized presence of the Risen Christ at our meals may be more formative of the life in Christ in us."

(*Living the Resurrection*, Eugene Peterson, 2006. Used by permission of NavPress, all rights reserved. www.navpress.com)

Day 4

" . . . so that all God's people may be thoroughly equipped for every good work" (2 Tim. 3:17).

Practice the Breath Prayer and/or your Heart Prayer in a posture that is comfortable for you.

Read and meditate on 1 Corinthians 10:27-11:1, *lectio divina* style. Then explore the following questions:
• What is Paul saying in this passage? How might that relate to our desire to connect with our neighbors?
• Of what value might accepting an invitation (and eating what's offered, v. 27, thanking God and enjoying it) be to your neighbor (v. 30)?
• How might we eat and drink to the glory of God?
• In what other ways might you apply verses 10:33 and 11:1?

Pray for opportunities to share meals as you seek to connect with your neighbors. Pray A-C-T-S for them by name.

Remember to pray your Heart Prayer regularly.

Day 5

" . . . so that all God's people may be thoroughly equipped for every good work" (2 Tim. 3:17).

Practice the Breath Prayer and/or your Heart Prayer in a posture that is comfortable for you.

Read Luke 9:11 and Acts 28:30-31 *lectio divina* style. Then explore the following questions:
- What's the common word in these passages?
- What did Jesus and Paul do? What else strikes you about these accounts?
- How can we welcome others into our homes, our groups, the church?
- Evaluate how welcoming you and your church are.

Remember to pray your Heart Prayer regularly.

LIFE STORY

A number of months ago, new neighbors moved in a few houses down the street from us. I saw a moving truck in the driveway, and that evening I rang the doorbell. I introduced myself, talked to the new owners about where they were moving from, and left them our phone number.

A week later, they knocked on my door around 9 p.m. They had changed the locks that day, but upon returning from an evening stroll they discovered that the lock had malfunctioned. Since it was getting cool out and they were all in T-shirts, I invited them to come for tea while they waited for some assistance. Finally around 10:30 p.m. they were able to get their door open and go home. In the meantime, I got to offer hospitality and get to know my new neighbors, who, though they don't believe in God, got to taste his hot tea. —MC

Day 6

" . . . so that all God's people may be thoroughly equipped for every good work" (2 Tim. 3:17).

Practice the Breath Prayer and/or your Heart Prayer in a posture that's comfortable for you.

Read and meditate on 1 Corinthians 13:1-7, *lectio divina* style. Then explore the following questions:
- What is love "greater than," according to verses 1-3?
- How well does society show that love is the greatest of all?
- How well do we (personally, as a group/neighborhood network, as a church) show that loving others is important?
- Give practical examples of how the characteristics of love identified in verses 4-7 apply to your life. (For example, "Love is patient when I have to wait in a traffic jam or checkout line" or "Love is kind when my sibling keeps pestering me.")
- What might love have to do with hospitality?

Choose one characteristic of love to demonstrate or work on this week in your relationships at home, at work or school, and in your neighborhood. Share your experience at your next group meeting.

Remember to pray your Heart Prayer regularly.

Day 7

" . . . so that all God's people may be thoroughly equipped for every good work" (2 Tim. 3:17).

Practice the Breath Prayer or the Heart Prayer in a posture that's comfortable for you.

Read and meditate on Matthew 15:32-39, *lectio divina* style. Then explore the following questions:
- Do you imagine Jesus as a hospitable person? Describe his character in this regard.

- What does this passage teach us about hospitality and God's part in it?
- How might God multiply our efforts to share a meal?

Praise (adore) God for his miracle-filled hospitality! Talk with God about how you want to partner with him in offering hospitality to those around you.

.

SERVING AND INVITING TO SERVE

Stories from the Journey

Sometimes it doesn't take much to show compassion or to serve your neighbors. Bring over a plate of cookies, a card, or some garden flowers or produce. Volunteer to take care of their pets, collect the mail, watch their place while they're away, shovel their walk and driveway while you're doing yours.

All of these little things build community—that sense of connectedness that we need. But sometimes a plate of cookies won't cut it. Sometimes your neighbors will find themselves in a real crisis or a difficult situation. That's where the rubber really meets the road.

Do you have a heart for people going through divorce, for people with mental or physical challenges, for addicts, abusers, wayward teens, those in financial crisis, the depressed, the lonely, the grieving? You'll find them in your very own neighborhood. And the difference in serving where you live is that you can't hop in your car and drive away and leave it behind like you do the soup kitchen or the halfway house. The challenge and the joy of serving in your community is that it's for the long haul. If you take the time to get to know and love your neighbors, you will also experience the privilege of serving them in times of need.

It's also a joy to join with neighbors in serving your city, your country, or a country far away. We've experienced this with our neighbors. Every time we got brave and put out a request ("Our kids are having a fundraiser to go to inner-city Los Angeles, Guatemala, Mexico . . . . would you like to make a donation, buy coffee, come to the silent auction?") our neighbors responded generously.

We had heard a number of "we should have a garage sale" comments from various neighbors as they began to ponder the task of spring cleanup. So we suggested that we have one big neighborhood yard sale. At one planning meeting, I mentioned that our family was going to donate our proceeds towards buying bikes for community workers in Zambia, a partnership our church was involved in. Before we knew it, everyone in the neighborhood was on board with that idea! We had a fabulous two days hanging out, sorting and telling stories about our junk, bartering, meeting other neighbors—and we ended up raising enough money to buy almost eleven bikes! We were a community with a mission, even though not all of us knew what that meant. God is great!

⬛ Sideward Pursuit (Group Meeting): Serve One Another

BEING COMMUNITY

"God has given each of you a gift from his great variety of spiritual gifts. Use them well to serve one another" (1 Peter 4:10).

Today, serve one another as you enjoy a meal together. In other words, don't let anyone serve themselves. Pour each other's coffee, carry each other's plates, clean up each other's mess. Then discuss the following questions:

• How does it feel to serve?

• How does it feel to be served?

• What did you learn from this little experiment?

Talk about your spiritual gifts (or the gifts that you *think* you have—see examples in 1 Cor. 12:4-11 and Rom. 12:6-8) and how they can be employed in the service of others.

Review Week 5
Review last week's material and discuss what you heard God saying about hospitality. Share with the group how you responded or will respond to that call.

Review and discuss the postures and practices for Week 5.

⬛ **Sideward:** How were you conscious of loving others this week?

⬆ **Upward:** Heart Prayers—share a few and tell how they impacted your days.

◀ Inward: Perseverance—when was this characteristic of Christ exhibited in you?

▶ Outward: Refrigerator rights—are you on the way to sharing them with your neighbors?

▣ Discuss This Week's Sideward Theme

"Each of you should use whatever give you have received to serve others, as faithful stewards of God's grace . . ." (1 Pet. 4:10).

Discuss the verse from 1 Peter and apply it your group and neighborhood contexts.

- How are the members of this group serving each other?
- What evidence have you already seen of your neighbors' desire to serve?
- Without violating confidentiality, share some of the needs in your neighborhood and brainstorm ways to serve.

Prepare for the Pursuits of the Week

Review and discuss the other postures and practices for Week 6.

▲ Upward: Surrender (A-C-T-S-S: Adoration, Confession, Thanksgiving, Supplication, and Surrender)

◀ Inward: Godliness

▶ Outward: Serve and Invite to Serve

Structure your communal prayer time around A-C-T-S-S. Invite everyone to express their prayers in short, simple sentences after a leader indicates each "heading" . . .

Triune God, we **adore** and praise you for . . .

Father, we **confess** . . . forgive . . .

Thank you, Lord, for . . .

(Supplication) . . . We pray for . . .

Dear God, we **surrender** our . . .

Practice the following upward, inward, and outward pursuits on your own this week. Plan to complete them before your next group meeting.

Upward Pursuit: **Surrender**

Read Romans 12:1-2 and 1 Samuel 3:10. As you continue with your devotional postures and practices this week, add a prayer of surrender ("Lord, I give you . . ." or "Lord, I surrender . . . to you").

Inward Pursuit: **Godliness**

"For this very reason, make every effort to add to your faith goodness; and to goodness, knowledge, and to knowledge, self-control; and to self-control, perseverance, and to perseverance, godliness . . ." (2 Pet. 1:5-6).

Being "godly" sounds presumptuous to some and unfathomable to others. Yet followers of Jesus are called and empowered to be like Jesus—and Jesus is godly.

Being godly or Christlike is a tall order, but thanks be to God that it's not all up to us. God's Spirit working in us conforms us more and more to the image of Christ, to *godliness*. God is the potter, we are the clay. In other words, it's more a matter of surrender than it is of making ourselves godly. Are you willing to be molded and made in God's own way?

Think about the following questions:

- Describe godliness. How does it describe/not describe you?
- What might you want to ask God to help you work on?
- What might be "dangerous" about being godly? How might others respond?

Think and pray about how you can and do reflect godliness in your neighborhood this week.

▶ Outward Pursuit: Serving and Inviting to Serve

"Religion that God our Father accepts as pure and faultless is this: to look after orphans and widows in their distress and keep oneself from being polluted by the world" (James 1:27).

It's time to get our hands dirty—or purified. How? By recognizing the needs of those in our neighborhoods and responding to them with simple and sometimes not-so-simple acts of service and compassion.

So here's your next challenge: Incorporate serving into your neighborhood life. Serve, show compassion, and invite others to participate.

Need some ideas? Start with a plate of cookies for the people coming in behind a moving truck, or a meal for the family with a new baby. Do some yardwork, housework, or minor repairs for a single parent, widow, or widower on your street. Plan a park cleanup day, or a "Love (your community's name) Day." Get others in your neighborhood involved too. Give them an opportunity to care, because they do care!

Discover what needs and concerns are on their hearts, and work together to address some of those issues. Gather some neighbors to volunteer with you on your next trip to the mission or the refugee center. I even know of a neighborhood group who took the neighborhood on an international mission trip!

- How have you served your neighbors?
- How could you serve them?
- How could you invite others to serve too?

LIFE STORY

As a recent widow, I really appreciate some help around the townhouse once in a while. I had e-mailed the pastor's wife with such a request, or so I thought. Her name happens to be the same as one of my neighbors and as it turns out I had e-mailed my neighbor—who responded right away, eager to help! That's how I learned again that most people love to give, and when we offer them that opportunity we are also blessing them! —LH

TIME WITH GOD'S WORD

Theme for the Week: Servants or Friends?

"If you keep my commands, you will remain in my love, just as I have kept my Father's commands and remain in his love. I have told you this that my joy may be in you and that your joy may be complete. My command is this: Love each other as I have loved you. Greater love has no one than this: to lay down one's life for one's friends. You are my friends if you do what I command. I no longer call you servants, because servants do not know their master's business. Instead, I have called you friends, for everything that I learned from my Father I have made known to you. You did not choose me, but I chose you and appointed you so that you might go and bear fruit—fruit that will last—and so that whatever you ask in my name the Father will give you. This is my command: Love each other" (John 15:10-17).

In God's kingdom, serving each other isn't always quite as simple as we might imagine. When we do good to others, there is always the danger that we will take the posture not of a servant, but of a "master." After all, we're the ones with the resources, the skills, the knowledge and expertise, the connections, the power and authority, right?

What does it mean that Jesus emptied himself? What does it really mean to serve? Can we ensure that our serving is good? Can we avoid the posture of "having" while approaching those who "have not"? What would it take for us to come alongside others as Jesus comes alongside us?

"I really don't think I can help a cause or community that I am not personally involved and invested in. If I'm not willing to share the community's fate (good or bad), how effective can I be? If I can insulate myself from the day-to-day realities; if I can step away (or move on) without personal consequences; if I can only sympathize and not empathize; I'm just a band-aid. A do-gooder who had the need to "pet the unfortunate" for a season—it makes you feel good, right? But if I'm buying what I'm selling, I have to truly walk in the community's shoes. And they aren't necessarily comfortable."

(posted 3/12/2007 on bgenis.blogspot.com)

Jesus gathers his followers together on the night he is to be betrayed. This is their last meal together. Jesus knows the end is near, so, like a parent on his deathbed, he wants to communicate the most important things to those gathered around him. He knows that these last words will be firmly imprinted in the minds and hearts of his followers. So what does he say? "You are my friends if you do what I command. I no longer call you servants, because servants do not know their master's business. Instead, I have called you friends, for everything that I learned from my Father I have made known to you."

Jesus really did and does have the power, the authority, the right to control and command. He is Lord of heaven and earth. And yet, he humbles himself and becomes a servant—washing feet, cleansing lepers, hanging out with sinners, caring for others with just the robe on his back. But he also invites us to be friends.

Friends come alongside. Friends are in relationship. Friends serve one another in community with mutual love and respect.

When we are the presence of Jesus in our neighborhoods, we're not just called to serve. We're called to be friends. Friends are people who we know and trust, care about, honor, value, and are committed to for the long haul. Friends give and receive, and help one another.

So go ahead and serve. Be kind, generous, and helpful in your neighborhood. But do more. Be a friend—the kind of friend who would lay down your life for another.

Day 2

"But those who look intently into the perfect law that gives freedom and continue in it—not forgetting what they have heard but doing it—they will be blessed in what they do" (James 1:25).

Practice the Breath Prayer or Heart Prayer in a posture that is comfortable for you.

Reflect on John 15:10-17, *lectio divina* style. Then explore the following questions:
- What did you highlight in the theme reflection? Why?
- What might God be saying to you, your group, or your church through it?
- If you were to apply the concept of being a friend to your life this week, what would that look like?
- Talk with God about what you're hearing, thinking, wrestling with, enjoying, and feeling called to do.

Day 3

"But those who look intently into the perfect law that gives freedom and continue in it—not forgetting what they have heard but doing it—they will be blessed in what they do" (James 1:25).

Practice the Breath Prayer or Heart Prayer in a posture that is comfortable for you.

Read and meditate on Matthew 25:35-40, *lectio divina* style. Then explore the following questions:
- How would you summarize the point of this passage?
- Who in your neighborhood context might be "the least of these"?

- What difference might it make if we imagined serving Jesus as we respond to the needs of those around us?
- Talk with God about what he wants you to learn and apply from this lesson.

Remember to pray for your neighbors and their needs this week.

Day 4

"But those who look intently into the perfect law that gives freedom and continue in it—not forgetting what they have heard but doing it—they will be blessed in what they do" (James 1:25).

Practice the Breath Prayer or Heart Prayer in a posture that is comfortable for you.

Read and meditate on 1 Corinthians 9:19-23, *lectio divina* style. Then explore these questions:
- How is Paul "living among"? Why?
- How do those in your neighborhood live? What common ground do you have with them? How can you live like them (be *in* the world but not *of* it)?
- How does Paul's passion and focus, as it is expressed in this passage (especially v. 23) compare with yours?
- What might your life look like if you did everything "for the sake of the gospel"?
- What might you have to surrender?

Pray the A-C-T-S-S prayer for yourself and your neighbors.

Day 5

"But those who look intently into the perfect law that gives freedom and continue in it—not forgetting what they have heard but doing it—they will be blessed in what they do" (James 1:25).

Practice the Breath Prayer or Heart Prayer in a posture that is comfortable for you.

Read and meditate on 1 Timothy 6:17-19, *lectio divina* style. Then explore the following questions:
- Would you consider yourself "rich in this world"? If so, what then does Paul want you to learn?
- Paul wants Christians to be "rich in good deeds" and "generous and willing to share." Does that describe you?

List several things that you could do, even today, to implement this directive. Choose one to do, and tell your group about it next time you meet.

Day 6

"But those who look intently into the perfect law that gives freedom and continue in it—not forgetting what they have heard but doing it—they will be blessed in what they do" (James 1:25).

Practice the Breath Prayer or Heart Prayer in a posture that is comfortable for you.

Read and meditate on John 13:1-17, *lectio divina* style. Then explore the following questions:
- As a disciple of Jesus, how have you experienced his love (v. 1), his authority (v. 3, 13), his washing (v. 4-10)?
- How have you/are you following his example?
- What might "foot washing" look like in your neighborhood?

Spend some more time with this text, and meditate on a verse or phrase that stands out for you. Talk with the Lord about it.

Pray the A-C-T-S-S prayer for yourself and your neighbors.

Day 7

"But those who look intently into the perfect law that gives freedom and continue in it—not forgetting what they have heard but doing it—they will be blessed in what they do" (James 1:25).

Practice the Breath Prayer or Heart Prayer in a posture that is comfortable for you.

Read and meditate on Matthew 9:35-38, *lectio divina* style. Then explore the following questions:
- What does this passage say Jesus did and felt?
- How can we imitate Jesus, announcing the good news about the kingdom where we are today?
- Do you think verse 37 is still true today? What will you do about it?
- How could you be a worker sent into the fields that are ready to be harvested in your neighborhood?

Pray the A-C-T-S-S prayer for yourself and your neighbors.

"DON'T INVITE THEM"

Stories from the Journey

Maybe it seems strange to you that the title of this book starts with a "don't." The whole book is about "do"—*do* intentionally, passionately, faithfully, and consistently pursue and engage in loving God, your neighbor, and one another. "Do this and live" (Luke 10:37).

Each week we have explored another aspect of "doing"— offering hospitality, serving, praying. But it's a doing that is intricately related to "being"—being neighbors, being occupied in our ordinary lives on ordinary days with the ordinary people with whom we live, being who we are: the light, salt, and sweet fragrance of the kingdom of God.

And then there's the word "invite." Don't invite? But isn't God all about inviting? He invites us to be in relationship with him; to partner with him on his mission; to know him intimately, personally, and communally, and invite others to do the same. Throughout this journey, we have been inviting neighbors into our homes, our families, our lives.

But there's the distinction. We have been inviting "them" to be *in relationship with* us—not to come to a program, an event, or a service. In church planting circles people often say, "If you build it, they won't come." Many of our neighbors are, for the most part, not interested in going to church. And if the statistics are true, a lot of those who claim to be Christian aren't too interested in it either. Church attendance is down across the continent. People are, however, interested in community, authenticity, and relationship. They are interested in making their lives and their communities better.

Then we get to the word "them." What if there is no such thing as "them"? What if it's all about us, *all of us*? What if God really does love everyone made in his image? What if he really did die for the *whole* world?

Why share our lives? In 1 Thessalonians 2:8, our theme verse for this week's Time with God's Word, Paul writes, "Because we loved you so much, we were delighted to share with you not only the gospel of God but our lives as well."

Why do we love our neighbors? Because Christ's love has moved us to do so. "His love has the first and last word in everything we do" (2 Cor. 5:14, *The Message*).

This past Christmas, we invited our neighbors to hear and tell the "traditional" Christmas story one evening. I photocopied the passages from Matthew and Luke and we gathered in our living room with food and drink, candles lit and carols playing softly. I began to read the story of God sending his own Son . . . and we paused and talked about angels and dreams. Then others volunteered to read . . . and we discussed what the star might have been (with some scientific terms that I don't comprehend). Then someone asked if we believed in the virgin birth, and I said, "Well, if you believe in angels, it might not be too farfetched to believe in the virgin birth as well."

I thanked God for my neighbors—from the three-year-olds to the seniors gathered there. You might say we were . . . church.

WEEK 7 PURSUITS ⬛ 🔼 ◀ ▶

⬛ Sideward Pursuit (Group Meeting): Encourage One Another

"Encourage one another and build each other up, just as in fact you are doing" (1 Thess. 5:11).

"Finally, brothers and sisters, rejoice! Strive for full restoration, encourage one another, be of one mind, live in peace. And the God of love and peace will be with you" (2 Cor. 13:11).

Being Community
Do something different to begin your gathering this week. For example, if you usually have dessert and coffee, go for appetizers and punch.

After you're done eating together, divide into teams. Just for fun, have each team list all the words they can think of that can be made using the letters in the word "encourage." Each word must have at least three letters, and no names of people or places are allowed. Give a round of applause to the team that comes up with the most!

Review Week 6
Review last week's material and discuss what you heard God saying. Also review the postures and practices for Week 6:
⬛ **Sideward:** How did you serve? How were you a friend?
🔼 **Upward:** What were the challenges and joys of surrendering?
◀ **Inward:** What were the challenges and joys of seeking to be godly?

▶ **Outward:** How are you doing on serving and inviting others to serve?

🗐 Discuss This Week's Sideward Theme

"Encourage one another and build each other up, just as in fact you are doing" (1 Thess. 5:11).

- Why is encouragement so important? How would you describe or define it?
- Share a time when you were encouraged, and a time when you found a way to encourage someone else.
- Write the name of each person in your group on a slip of paper and place the slips in a hat or basket. Have everyone take one slip. This week, encourage the person whose name you drew. Send encouraging notes; intercede for him or her; meet for coffee to talk about where that person feels the need for encouragement.
- But don't keep all that encouragement to yourselves! On the back of the slip you drew, write the name of a neighbor whom you will encourage in the same way this week. Be attentive to the Spirit's promptings. Perhaps you will have opportunity to ask the person what they would like God to do for them at this time, and then you can pray and talk about those concerns specifically.

Prepare for the Pursuits of the Week

Review and discuss the other postures and practices for Week 7.

⬆ **Upward** and ▶ **Outward**: Exegetical Prayer Walk—talk about how to do this together or separately.

◀ **Inward:** Mutual Affection—discuss the questions together.

Pray for one another. You might close with the words of 2 Corinthians 13:11, each inserting the name of the person on your left as you say it together:

> May [name] be joyful. May [he/she] continue to grow to maturity. May [he/she] encourage others and be encouraged. May [he/she] live in harmony and peace in [her/his]

neighborhood. And may the God of love and peace be with [name].

Practice the following upward, inward, and outward pursuits on your own this week. Plan to complete them before your next group meeting.

⬆ Upward and ➡ Outward Pursuit: Exegetical Prayer Walk

This week's upward pursuit and outward pursuit are combined into one challenge: exegeting and praying for your neighborhood by exploring it on foot. You can do this alone or with someone else who lives in your neighborhood.

To exegete is to "critically interpret," as we do when we study the Bible, seeking to discern what it means and how it applies to our lives. In this exercise you're invited to undertake an exegesis— a critical interpretation—of your neighborhood.

You will need to set aside about two hours (more or less, depending on the size of your neighborhood) so that you can take your time—exploring, pausing, discerning, praying.

Through careful, sensitive, and critical observation, your task is to discern the truth of God's presence where you live. As you do that, talk with God about what you're seeing, hearing, and learning, and intercede on behalf of the people you encounter along the way.

If you've never participated in a prayer walk before, here are a few tips:

1. **Sketch out your neighborhood.** Before you go anywhere, draw (or obtain) a map of your neighborhood. Include the homes on your street with the names of the residents if possible, street patterns, landmarks such as parks, shops, churches, schools, and other community buildings. Be sure to include boundary markers or natural borders that define your neigh-

borhood. This will help you set the parameters of your route, which has to be walkable. Sketch out your route (but be flexible, because once you are on your way it may change!). Note that the scope of this exercise is likely larger than your S-A-F-E context as defined in Week 1, but it might not be. You might want to continue to focus simply on your block, depending on whether other Christ-followers in your neighborhood are joining you on the journey or not.

2. **Pray and prepare for your mission.** Bring your neighborhood map, good walking shoes, a notebook, a pen, a photocopy of the prayer walk questions and suggestions that follow, and a little cash in case you want to pause with someone for coffee along the way. Most important, bring an open mind, a gracious heart, and an attentive spirit. Before you go, pray this prayer:

Breathe on me, breath of God, breathe on me. Give me your eyes to see this community and its people as you do. Give me your ears to listen to their hearts as you hear them. Give me an open and attentive spirit to recognize where you are already at work. Fill me with courage that I might ask the right questions, accept the true answers, and follow your leading. Equip and empower me to engage in this place, to live among people as you did, Lord Jesus, giving it all. Amen.

3. **Step out.** As you walk, consider and make note of the following things:
   - On average, how old are the residences in your neighborhood? How much renovation or rebuilding is going on?
   - Do gardens and yards look well cared for? What do you notice about the front entrances?
   - Are there many places for sale or rent? What evidence do you see of transience or permanence?
   - Does the area adjoin a major highway or a commercial, industrial, or business area?
   - What was here before this neighborhood? What has been gained or lost over the years?

- If there are community and civic buildings, what are they for? How do they appear (well-used, unkempt)? How do they feel (friendly, inviting, scary)?
- How are the public spaces being used? By whom? Are they adequate?
- If there are shops or other commercial spaces, who is the clientele? Is there space to relax, chat, pause?
- The local park/playground/green space . . . what do you notice about it? Does it feel like an inviting place? Who is there? How is it used?
- What is missing in your neighborhood?
- Do you have any other thoughts, feelings, or observations?

4. **Pause and pray.**
- At the end of each street, ask God's blessing on the residents (if you know them by name, all the better).
- At schools, pray for students and teachers.
- At churches, pray for their ministry, staff, and mission.
- At businesses, pray for integrity, success, and fair, honest business practices.
- At fire hydrants, pray for firefighters. At street lights, for police officers. At stop signs, for safe streets. At bus stops, for city workers and commuters.
- As people pass by, pray for them.
- You get the idea. Follow where the Spirit leads!

5. **Stop and sit.** At a cafe, on a tree-lined street, or on a park bench, take a break.
- What are the sights, sounds, and smells of your neighborhood?
- Are there places that feel unsafe—places where you wouldn't normally go?
- Are there places of hope, beauty, community?
- Chat with those around you . . . if you're really brave, ask them if they live in the neighborhood and what they think are its strengths and struggles.

- Continue on your walk, returning to your starting point when you're finished.

6. **Reflect and discern.** After your walk is over, take some time to think or talk with your group about the following questions:
   - What it would be like to live in this neighborhood if you were house-bound, single, disadvantaged, without a vehicle, very young, or very old?
   - Did you see evidence of struggle, despair, neglect, and alienation?
   - What's your sense of the community's state of mind? Is it dominated by fear and anxiety, longing and hopefulness, joy and contentment, friendliness and security?
   - How did you sense God's presence and activity in your neighborhood?
   - What else did you learn or discern?
   - How will you respond?

Share your experiences with your group, especially your reflections.

7. **Make a plan to try it again**—Try the whole experience again with a partner or two from your neighborhood network or small group. You might also plan to repeat the prayer walk every six months or so and then see how your perceptions have changed, what else you discover, how you can pray more specifically.

Inward Pursuit: Mutual Affection

"For this very reason, make every effort to add to your faith goodness; and to goodness, knowledge; and to knowledge, self-control; and to self-control, perseverance; and to perseverance, godliness; and to godliness, mutual affection" (2 Pet. 1:5-7).

In *The Message*, Eugene Peterson interprets the phrase "mutual affection" as "warm friendliness." So what does warm friendliness have to do with being conformed to the image of Christ?

Good question. It sounds like the "greet each other with a holy kiss" kind of thing. The response I usually hear to that directive is "Do we *have* to?" But what if there is more to mutual affection than we might at first imagine? What if there is more to the Trinity than what Theology 101 has led us to believe? What if Father, Son, and Spirit *are* mutually affectionate?

Whatever its shortcomings, the recent bestseller *The Shack* illustrates this beautifully. Spirit, Father, Son love to be together. They model a close, authentic, tender, attentive, *mutually affectionate* relationship. When we add mutual affection to our faith, goodness, knowledge, self-control, and godliness, we become more like our triune God—and others take notice.

Take a minute to think about these questions:

- What does mutual affection look like for you? How do you greet your spouse, other family members, close friends, fellow journeyers? How might God want you to stretch and grow in this regard?
- How does your small group greet each other each week? Could you express more mutual affection, keeping in mind individual comfort zones? How?
- How could you leave your comfort zone and exhibit "warm friendliness" this week?

TIME WITH GOD'S WORD

Theme for the Week: Share Your Life *and* the Gospel

"Because we loved you so much, we were delighted to share with you not only the gospel of God but our lives as well" (1 Thess. 2:8).

Read the following two stories.

Story 1: I found out that my Muslim neighbors went to a community church for two years when they lived in Ontario and that she still keeps in touch with two of her good friends who are Christians. I also found out that when their son was born, it was her Christian friends who were at the hospital with her because her husband was working out of town. After her baby was born, they prayed over him and she was totally okay with it. She told me she has a Christian Bible and that they would be open to attending a community church but they are not allowed to go to churches where you make the sign of the cross and she doesn't like churches that are rigid and tell you what to do. She explained that she believed in Jesus and Mohammed and two other guys. I invited her to tell me more sometime, as I really don't know too much about it. It was awesome! And it was all because I offered her some of the cantaloupe and broccoli that was left over from church camp and was willing to stop and visit. —KS

Story 2: God has impressed on me in many ways that I need to continue to connect with my neighbors. On Sunday evening after I got home, I cut a bunch of Swiss chard out of my garden. I like to give produce away to bless people around me, and it gives me a way to connect with them. I went next door with the Swiss chard and got talking with my neighbor and her friend, who I ended up giving a lift home because of a sudden storm. On the way, she shared with me her multiple stories of loss. I was able to pray with her and pass on some contact information. Wow, God is full of surprises and blessings when we step out for, and with him—and give him the space and the time to do his work! —CN

These two stories have something in common: the willingness on the part of those who love the Lord to also love their neighbors by being there, by listening, and by taking the time for relationship. They all made space for moments and they all took the risk of engaging in conversations and being open and honest about their other friend, Jesus. When we do that, that posture changes people's assumptions about church, God, Jesus, faith, and what it means to be a follower of Christ. That's evangelism!

The book *The Tangible Kingdom* by Hugh Halter and Matt Smay includes this insightful quote: "I've concluded that, almost without exception, relationships are formed, important dialogue and conversation begin and powerful moments of ministry occur during spontaneous, unplanned moments while we are sharing our lives together. . . . Over time, I have learned that 'interruptions' are the very place where I look for God to work" (Jossey-Bass, p.161).

It seems to me that dealing with "interruptions" was a major part of Jesus' work on earth. The big-crowd teachings and healings were great, but the stories that stand out for me—the moments that changed lives and communities—were "chance" encounters. For example, Jesus stops by a well for a rest and meets a Samaritan woman whose whole village comes to believe (John 4). Or Jesus is walking along and "happens" to notice Zacchaeus in a tree, then goes to his house for dinner, after which Zacchaeus gives half of his possessions away (Luke 19).

So what does this mean for you and me as we try to love our neighbors? It invites us to develop rhythms of sharing life, of being available and present so that these powerful moments can happen! We have to be intentional about having space, time, and energy to truly live *with* our neighbors. Because if we're not taking time to be there, guess what? We won't be there.

During a recent time of insane busyness around a community event, a neighbor friend invited us to an "after party" party. Truth be told, going to another party wasn't what I had had in mind; it was Saturday night and already late. But a little voice inside me said, "Get over it, sweetheart, and go."

So I went, and I was there for the moment that God chose to open the door for a deep spiritual conversation with a hurting man whose wife had had an affair. He had a chance to share his heart and be heard. We talked about his divorce, his daughters, and Jesus. We talked about him having belief and wanting his girls to have it too. God had a moment with that man, and I got to be a part of it. There's nothing more amazing!

It's not always easy, but those moments of simply "being there" are often the times when God uses us to bring his love to our neighbors.

Day 2

"The farmer plants seed by taking God's word to others" (Mark 4:14, New Living Translation).

Pray the Breath Prayer or the Heart Prayer in a posture that feels comfortable to you.

Read 1 Thessalonians 2:6-12, *lectio divina* style. Then explore the following questions:
- Underline all the phrases that describe how Paul and his team acted among the Thessalonians. What strikes you about this list? Does it sound *loving*?
- What might this kind of living look like in your neighborhood?
- If you were to write a letter to your neighborhood five years from now, what would it say? Or what would you *like* it to say?

- What did you note in the theme reflection that inspired you? Equipped you? Urged you?
- What will you do this week to "share your life"?

Write and pray a Heart Prayer based on your reflections today.

Day 3

"The farmer plants seed by taking God's word to others" (Mark 4:14, New Living Translation).

Pray the Breath Prayer or the Heart Prayer in a posture that feels comfortable to you.

Read and meditate on John 16:13-15, *lectio divina* style. Then explore the following questions:
- What does Jesus say the Spirit will do for his followers?
- How do you respond to these words?
- How do Acts 11:28 and 19:21 illustrate this?
- When or how have you felt the prompting and leading of the Spirit?
- Why might that be important as you nurture connections with your neighbors?

Day 4

"The farmer plants seed by taking God's word to others" (Mark 4:14, New Living Translation).

Pray the Breath Prayer or the Heart Prayer in a posture that feels comfortable to you.

Read Acts 9:10-19, *lectio divina* style. Then explore the following questions:
- Imagine that you are Ananias. What are you thinking and feeling? How would you describe your/his "posture"? How did

you/Ananias react to the discovery that God was working in Saul's (your enemy's) life?

- What's amazing to you about this story? What is unsettling? What if Saul lived in your neighborhood?
- Does God still lead people in this way? How?
- What "scales" might be blinding people in your neighborhood context?
- How might God want to use you to help remove them? Consider what you observed on your exegetical prayer walk.
- How might you be led and used by God in your neighborhood context this week?
- Talk with God about this story and its application for you.

Day 5

"The farmer plants seed by taking God's word to others" (Mark 4:14, New Living Translation).

Pray the Breath Prayer or the Heart Prayer in a posture that feels comfortable to you.

Read and meditate on Romans 8:14-17, 26-30, *lectio divina* style. Then explore the following questions:
- What does the Spirit do for and in us?
- How has the Spirit been working in you—
  to assure you that you are a child and heir of God (vv. 16-17)?
  to help you in your weakness (8:26)?
  to keep you in harmony with God's own will (8:27)?
  to cause everything to work together for good (8:28)?
- What in these texts makes you feel confident?

Pray with the Spirit for those in your neighborhood context.

Day 6

"The farmer plants seed by taking God's word to others" (Mark 4:14, New Living Translation).

Pray the Breath Prayer or the Heart Prayer in a posture that feels comfortable to you.

Read and meditate on 2 Timothy 4:1-5, 17, *lectio divina* style. Then explore the following questions:

- What are Timothy and you urged to do?
- How is our time like or unlike the time Paul describes? How does that impact how we live out this text?
- How do we work at telling others the good news and fully carrying out the ministry God has given us (v. 5)?
- What ministry has God given you right where you are?

Use your thoughts from this passage to shape your A-C-T-S-S prayer today.

"If we can only 'touch heaven' by experiencing something spiritually new, or spiritually sentimental, then we have missed the point of walking with Jesus or living an incarnational life. . . . I am constantly being corrected by the Lord to stop seeking after the ecstatic experiences in order to hear him and see him at work, but to look for him in the mundane, and in the midst of real life experiences and events."

("Naturally Being Supernatural" by Don Davis, posted on "The Dreaming Revolutionary," www.dondavis.wordpress.com)

Day 7

"The farmer plants seed by taking God's word to others" (Mark 4:14, New Living Translation).

Pray the Breath Prayer or the Heart Prayer in a posture that feels comfortable to you.

Read and meditate on Mark 2:1-12 (especially vv. 1-5), *lectio divina* style. Then explore the following questions:

- Describe the four men. What were they determined to do? Why do you think they were so determined?
- What "roof tiles" might you need to remove in order to get closer to Jesus? How?
- Have in mind one specific person in your missional context whom you really care about. What is the "mat" that would help him/her get nearer to Jesus?
- Who are you partnering with in your neighborhood or missional context to help with the "carrying" and "roof removal"?
- How much effort are you willing to put into bringing your friend closer to Jesus?

PEOPLE OF PEACE

In 1 Corinthians 12, Paul emphasizes that the body of Christ has many members or "parts." Each part has its unique giftedness and usefulness. But being incarnational and missional in our approach to the neighborhood means joining with other "body parts" in order to be the fully functioning body of Christ in the neighborhood.

If you don't know everyone in your neighborhood, how do you go about finding the other members of Christ's body where you live? One strategy is to stay home one Sunday morning and observe who leaves for church. Another person in our group sent an invitation to prayer to the people who lived within a few blocks of her home. (She got no response, but it was a great idea!)

Here's another idea. A while back, we planned a big block party with our neighbors. We distributed flyers to about sixty homes. We had our city permit and roadblock barriers. We lined up a "jumpy thing," pony rides, grills, coolers, lawn chairs, street chalk. We planned some "get to know you" activities. We also had special nametags. In addition to writing their names, people had to complete five sentences about themselves, such as "I'm a . . . ." and "I belong to . . . ."

Thanks to the nametags, we discovered other followers of Jesus in our neighborhood. One man had written "I'm a pastor" on his nametag. Others listed an affiliation with a denomination. We took note of those folks, and started gathering with them occasionally. We eat a meal together, meditate on Scripture, pray, learn, and are committed to loving our neighbors and making our neighborhood an even better place to live. For those who participate, a new understand of God's kingdom is opening up before our eyes!

One participant who is a pastor remarked the other day, "I've been working in the church with church people for years. For the first time I feel like I am actually doing the Great Commission." I understood what he was talking about.

As I write this, our group has committed to pray by name for our neighbors for twenty-eight days. We have each taken responsibility for covering our own street in prayer. As we do this, we've seen God using us by opening our hearts to others and opening connections with people in whose hearts he is already at work.

We aren't "there" yet, but we're on the journey. It's not always easy, but it truly has been a joy! We're enjoying getting to know each other as brothers and sisters in Christ, sharing what we see God doing, and partnering with God to make a difference where he has placed us. We are awed by the wonder, joy, and privilege of experiencing God's kingdom right here in our neighborhood—on earth as it is in heaven.

⬇ Sideward Pursuit (Group Meeting): Lay Down Your Lives for One Another

"This is how we know what love is: Jesus Christ laid down his life for us. And we ought to lay down our lives for one another" (1 John 3:16).

Being Community
Enjoy a meal together and share stories of times when you experienced "good community."

Review Week 7
Review the postures and practices for Week 7.

⬇ **Sideward:** How did you encourage another person last week?

⬅ **Inward:** What were the challenges and joys of showing mutual affection?

⬆ **Upward** and ➡ **Outward:** Share your prayer walk experiences and reflections. What were the highlights? What did you discover, discern, appreciate? How did the prayer walk impact your understanding of God and your neighborhood or missional context?

After each person has had time to share, allow time for others in the group to tell what they appreciated about his or her story.

⬇ Discuss This Week's Sideward Theme
Our theme for this week is a call to lay down our lives for one another—to live sacrificially for the sake of others and for Jesus'

sake. This is the core of what it means to follow Jesus, who laid down his life for us.

Discuss these questions together:
- What does it mean to "lay down your life" for another person?
- How do we *really* live that out as individuals and as a group?
- How does "laying down your life" connect with our inward pursuit of love this week?

Prepare for the Pursuits of the Week
Review and discuss the other postures and practices for Week 8.
- ⬆ **Upward:** Reverence and Intimacy—how is this helpful for your relationship with God?
- ◀ **Inward:** Love
- ▶ **Outward:** Communitas

This is your last group meeting. You have completed eight weeks of keeping Christ's command to "love your neighbor as yourself." Talk about next steps together. Do you want to keep meeting as a group? (If so, the resource list at the end of this guidebook contains suggestions for further reading and study that your group could do together.) Talk about your future goals for your neighborhood.

If you like, plan a wrap-up celebration: enjoy a special meal, make a banner, light some fireworks, laugh, tell stories, and enjoy each others' company. And most of all, thank God for leading you into neighborhood life.

Practice the following upward, inward, and outward pursuits on your own this week.

Upward Pursuit: **Reverence and Intimacy**

"Love the Lord your God with all your heart and with all your soul and with all your mind and with all your strength" (Mark 12:30).

Over the past two months, we have been challenged and equipped to keep the first and greatest commandment through a number of different postures and practices. Think about these questions as you reflect on your experience:

- How has your love for God grown?
- Which postures and practices helped you to connect with God best? Reflect on and talk with God about them.
    Breath Prayers
    Open Hands
    Lectio Divina
    A-C-T-S-S
    Heart Prayers
    Exegetical Prayer Walking

In *The Message*, Eugene Peterson shows how the two Marys expressed both reverence and intimacy when they saw the risen Jesus:

The women, deep in wonder and full of joy, lost no time in leaving the tomb. They ran to tell the disciples. Then Jesus met them, stopping them in their tracks. "Good morning!" he said. They fell to their knees, embraced his feet, and worshiped him (Matt. 28:8-9).

They fell to their knees (an act of reverence), embraced his feet (an act of intimacy) and worshiped him (another act of reverence). When you think about your relationship with God, how can or do you express both reverence and intimacy?

Inward Pursuit: **Love**

"His divine power has given us everything we need for a godly life through our knowledge of him who called us by his own glory and goodness. Through these he has given us his very great and precious promises, so that through them you may participate in the divine nature, having escaped the corruption in the world caused by evil desires. For this very reason, make every effort to add to your faith goodness; and to goodness, knowledge; and to knowledge, self-control; and to self-control, perseverance; and to perseverance, godliness; and to godliness, mutual affection; and to mutual affection, love. For if you possess these qualities in increasing measure, they will keep you from being ineffective and unproductive in your knowledge of our Lord Jesus Christ" (2 Peter 1:3-8).

Love God . . . love your neighbor . . . love one another . . . love your enemies. In the Bible we read about love over and over again. We talk about it. We believe in it. We're all for it. But do we do it? Do we love unconditionally and unceasingly? Do we lay down our lives for one another?

Seek to make love the verb that characterizes your life this week.

▶ Outward Pursuit: **Communitas**

Over the last eight weeks, we have not only been building a sense of community but a sense of *communitas*: community with a mission. By now you know what your final challenge is: to be a *communitas* in your neighborhood context with others who live there.

Intentionality is a key word for continuing the journey of loving our neighbors and being a neighborhood *communitas*. That's what it will take to build *communitas* over the long haul.

So pull out your household calendar and make a plan for the coming month.

- Which neighbors will you have over, when, for what?
- Can you commit to a weekly meal (or two) with neighbors?
- When will you do another prayer walk down your street?
- How will you begin (or continue) to develop a neighborhood network or *communitas*?
- Which sideward, upward, inward, and outward pursuits will you continue to follow, and how?

TIME WITH GOD'S WORD

Theme for the Week: *Communitas*

So what's wrong with thinking that our mission is to invite people to church? When that's our goal, we expect the church to provide people with services, meet their needs, and bring them to Jesus. Identifying church this way makes it into an institution, a staff, a building, a program, a service provider that we can choose to consume from or not.

But the Bible describes the church as the people of God, or the community of God with a mission. The biblical word for church is *ecclesia*, meaning "called-out ones." We are called out, not to leave something, but *to love* and to be God's presence where we are.

As Simon Carey Holt puts it, "God's call is a call to place. He calls us into particular places that we can see, walk, smell and inhabit. God's call is not a call to be everywhere; it's a call to be somewhere. . . . It's a call to locality . . . it's a call to the neighborhood" (*God Next Door: Spirituality and Mission in the Neighbourhood*, p. 77).

That is what the church was made and meant to be, and that is what we find in the New Testament: a community of Jesus' followers with the mission of bringing God's blessing where they live. As Abraham was blessed to be a blessing to the whole world (Gen. 12:2), we are meant to be a blessing not just to each other but to our neighborhoods. That's the difference between the church striving to be a community unto itself (that we go to and invite others to) and the church being *communitas* in the neighborhood and the world.

Of course, we all long for community. We were made for relationship! But to pursue it for its own sake leaves us with pseudo-community. In contrast, the triune God is a picture of perfect community, love, harmony, wholeness, holiness, and *mission*. By God's very nature, God is always extending himself, always being hospitable to the world he made. God is community and mission. That's the model for the church's life.

"Communitas, in the way I want to define it, is a community infused with a grand sense of purpose; a purpose that lies outside of its current internal reality and constitution. It's the kind of community that 'happens' to people in actual pursuit of a common vision of what could be. It involves movement and it describes the experience of togetherness that only really happens among a group of people actually engaging in a mission outside itself."

Being *communitas* and loving our neighbors isn't about offering people a ticket to heaven. It's about creating the space in and through our living together for all of us to participate with God in the telling of his Story. It's about helping others encounter Jesus and his love. It's about discovering meaning and purpose for life *now*, because God has already won the victory—and moved into the neighborhood.

Day 2

"But these are written that you may believe that Jesus is the Messiah, the Son of God, and that by believing you may have life in his name" (John 20:31).

Using one of the practices you have learned, pray with reverence and intimacy.

Think and pray about your response to the theme for the week.
- As you think about the text and the theme reflections, what stands out for you? Why?
- How would you describe the distinction between community and *communitas*, as the term is used here?

- Finish this sentence, "One thing I want to remember and think more about is . . . ."

Day 3

"But these are written that you may believe that Jesus is the Messiah, the Son of God, and that by believing you may have life in his name" (John 20:31).

Using one of the practices you have learned, pray with reverence and intimacy.

Read John 12:23-28a, *lectio divina* style. This might seem like a strange passage to include in a study of *communitas,* because we often apply it in a more personal or individualistic way. But what if, as Peter Bush suggests in his book *In Dying We Are Born*, there is a sense that the church too—its groups and programs, its ways of doing things—also has to die in order to experience resurrection? Only God can accomplish that.

Read verses 23-26 several times and explore these questions:
- How is the Son of Man glorified? Do you think that applies to those who follow him as well?
- What grains of wheat might have to die for a plentiful harvest of new lives to be produced in your life? In your group? In your church?
- What is Jesus saying to you in verse 26?

Read John 12:27-28. Make the first part of verse 28 your heart prayer for the day: "Father, glorify your name!"

Day 4

"But these are written that you may believe that Jesus is the Messiah, the Son of God, and that by believing you may have life in his name" (John 20:31).

Using one of the practices you have learned, pray with reverence and intimacy.

Read Luke 14:25-35, *lectio divina* style. Then explore the following questions:
- What is the cost of being Jesus' disciple?
- Are you ready to pay it? Take your time in answering this question.
- What do the last two verses of this passage have to do with the rest of Jesus' message here?
- How would you connect this passage with the theme of *communitas*?
- How will you carry your cross and follow Jesus in your neighborhood today?

Pray that God will B-L-E-S-S your neighbors.

Day 5

"But these are written that you may believe that Jesus is the Messiah, the Son of God, and that by believing you may have life in his name" (John 20:31).

Using one of the practices you have learned, pray with reverence and intimacy.

Read 1 Corinthians 9:24-27, *lectio divina* style. Then explore the following questions:
- What does "discipline" look like in your spiritual life?
- How are you going to continue maturing and growing in your faith and your commitment to your neighborhood?
- What would help you make that happen? What would hinder you?

Pray A-C-T-S-S for your neighborhood, including you and your family.

Day 6

"But these are written that you may believe that Jesus is the Messiah, the Son of God, and that by believing you may have life in his name" (John 20:31).

Using one of the practices you have learned, pray with reverence and intimacy.

Read 1 Timothy 2:1-6, *lectio divina* style. Then explore the following questions:
- What does Paul urge Timothy to do and why?
- What strikes you about Paul's expression of the Good News in this text?

Pray for each person on your neighborhood list using phrases from these verses. For example: "Thank you, God, that you want (name) to be saved. May he know that you are the only true God. . . ."

Day 7

"But these are written that you may believe that Jesus is the Messiah, the Son of God, and that by believing you may have life in his name" (John 20:31).

Using one of the practices you have learned, pray with reverence and intimacy.

Read 2 Timothy 1:3-14, *lectio divina* style. Then explore the following questions:
- What in these verses highlights the idea of *communitas*?
- How does Paul describe the Spirit God has given you?
- Describe, define, or journal about the three positive traits of the Spirit.
- Can you tell others about the Lord without feeling "ashamed" (v. 8)?
- What makes being open about your faith difficult for you?

Pray for opportunities to share your faith with others, and be attentive to God's promptings.

Consider memorizing verse 7 and repeating it throughout the day: "For the Spirit God gave us does not make us timid, but gives us power, love and self-discipline."

Now that you're at the end of this guidebook, think about how you can incorporate the sideward, upward, inward, and outward pursuits in your daily living.

Resources

Publications

Bosch, David. *Transforming Mission*. Orbis Books, 1991.

Boren, Scott. *The Relational Way: From Small Group Structures to Holistic Life Connections*. Touch, 2007.

Bowen, John. *Evangelism for "Normal" People*. Augsburg Fortress, 2002.

Bush, Peter. *In Dying We Are Born: The Challenge and the Hope for Congregations*. Alban, 2007.

Callahan, Kennon L. *Small, Strong Congregations: Creating Strengths and Health for your Congregation*. Jossey-Bass, 2000.

Choung, James. *True Story: A Christianity Worth Believing In*. IVP, 2008.

deVries, John F. *Praying the Lord's Prayer for Neighbors: A House of Prayer Devotional Guide*. Hope Ministries, 1999.

Frazee, Randy. *The Connecting Church: Beyond Small Groups to Authentic Community*. Zondervan, 2001.

Frost, Michael. *Exiles: Living Missionally in a Post-Christian Culture*. Hendrickson, 2006.

Frost, Michael and Alan Hirsch: *ReJesus: A Wild Messiah for a Missional Church*. Hendrickson, 2008.

Halter, Hugh and Matt Smay. *The Tangible Kingdom: Creating Incarnational Community*. Jossey-Bass, 2008.

Halter, Hugh and Matt Smay. *Tangible Kingdom Primer: An Eight-Week Guide to Incarnational Community*. Missio, 2009.

Hirsch, Alan. *The Forgotten Ways: Reactivating the Missional Church*. Brazos Press, 2007.

Hirsch, Alan and Darryn Altclass. *The Forgotten Ways Handbook: A Practical Guide for Developing Missional Churches*. Brazos Press, 2009.

Holt, Simon Carey. *God Next Door: Spirituality and Mission in the Neighbourhood*. Acorn Press (Australia), 2007.

Hybels, Bill. *Just Walk Across the Room: Simple Steps Pointing People to Faith*. Zondervan, 2006.

Myers, Joseph. *The Search to Belong.* Zondervan, 2003

Payne, J. D. *Missional House Churches.* Paternoster, 2008.

Peterson, Eugene. *Living the Resurrection: The Risen Christ in Everyday Life.* NavPress, 2006.

Rouse, Rick and Craig Van Gelder. *A Field Guide to the Missional Congregation: Embarking on a Journey of Transformation.* Augsburg, 2008.

Roxburgh, Alan and M. Scott Boren. *Introducing the Missional Church: What It Is, Why It Matters, How to Become One.* Baker Books, 2009.

Roxburgh, Alan and Fred Romaniuk. *The Missional Leader: Equipping Your Church to Reach a Changing World.* Jossey-Bass, 2006.

Stetzer, Ed and David Putman. *Breaking the Missional Code: Your Church Can Become a Missionary in Your Community.* B&H Academic, 2006.

Stetzer, Ed and Philip Nation. *Compelled by Love: The Most Excellent Way to Missional Living.* New Hope, 2008.

Van Gelder, Craig. *The Missional Church in Context.* Eerdmans, 2007.

Van Gelder, Craig. *The Ministry of the Missional Church: A Community Led by the Spirit* Baker, 2007.

Organizations

Christian Reformed Home Missions offers a course called "Everyday Evangelism". Visit www.crhm.org or call 800-266-2175 for more information.

Forge Canada is a growing network of leaders and churches in Canada who are committed to training leaders and churches to transform their neighbourhoods—MTN (Missional Training Network) or N3 (Neighbourhood Network Night, www.forgecanada.ca.